EXCEL VBA

ED ROBINSON

BARNES
&NOBLE
BOOKS
NEW YORK

In easy steps is an imprint of Computer Step
Southfield Road . Southam
Warwickshire CV47 0FB . United Kingdom
www.ineasysteps.com

This edition published for Barnes & Noble Books, New York
FOR SALE IN THE USA ONLY
www.bn.com

Notice of Liability
Every effort has been made to ensure that this book contains
accurate and current information. However, Computer Step and the
author shall not be liable for any loss or damage suffered by readers
as a result of any information contained herein.

Trademarks
Microsoft® and Windows® are registered trademarks of Microsoft
Corporation. All other trademarks are acknowledged as belonging to
their respective companies.

Printed and bound in the United Kingdom

ISBN 0-7607-5732-1

Contents

Getting started

In this chapter, we will see that Excel VBA is fun, and simple to learn.

Why learn Excel VBA? We will consider this question and then learn to write, run and edit our first program.

Covers

Chapter One

Introduction

Why learn Excel VBA?

Excel Visual Basic for Applications extends and customizes Excel – allowing us to do things that Excel itself is not able to do.

For those who simply wish to learn to program, Excel is an ideal environment. The spreadsheet is well suited as a programming interface – for inputting data to be processed as well as displaying the results.

It is not essential to make a further software purchase in order to learn the elements of Visual Basic programming. Excel VBA comes free of charge with every copy of Excel (97, 2000, 2002, 2003, etc.) and provides a great deal of the functionality of stand-alone Visual Basic – and more!

There may be some with financial/accounting experience who have come to realize that simply recording a macro has limitations, and that it is necessary to start to learn Excel VBA from the ground up. Excellent texts abound, but where to start?

Just because Excel VBA is easy to learn, does not mean that it is not a serious programming language. It can also be used to perform complex tasks such as automatically getting up-to-date financial information from the Internet, or calculating option prices. It is even used in scientific applications.

One of the great advantages of Excel VBA is the macro recorder (which stand-alone Visual Basic does not have). This is invaluable if you are struggling with some programming syntax. Just get the recorder to do it for you and then view the code to see how it is done! We will learn about the macro recorder in Chapter 5.

There are many ways to write a program using Excel VBA. We could write user-defined functions (which are a type of bespoke worksheet function), in which we could try our experimental code, or we could record a macro and place our trial code in it. Each has advantages and disadvantages. For the most part, we will place our experimental code inside a command button procedure. We will now describe that method, and learn just how easy it is to program in Excel VBA.

Writing your first program

We will place a command button on a sheet which we can click in order to run a simple program.

Firstly, in order to draw a button on our sheet, we need the Control Toolbox.

1   Click <u>V</u>iew, <u>T</u>oolbars, and then Control Toolbox.

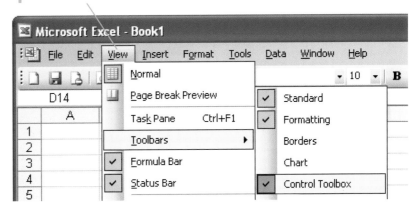

2   Click the Design Mode button. This step is not essential!

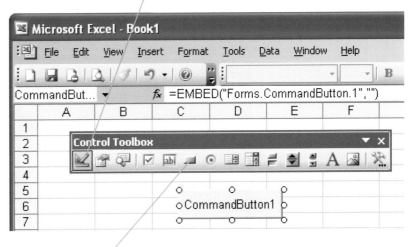

You can reposition the command button by clicking on it and dragging. You can resize it by dragging the sizing handles.

3   Click the Command Button on the Control Toolbox, click on the sheet and then drag a command button on the sheet as shown.

4 In order to view the code editor, click on the View Code button.

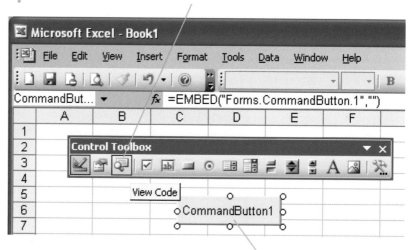

Alternatively, double-click on the command button making sure that the Design Mode button is still depressed.

5 The Visual Basic Editor (VBE) appears. Click inside this "code skeleton" to place the cursor here.

Other windows may appear in the VBE application window as well – for example, the Project Explorer window.

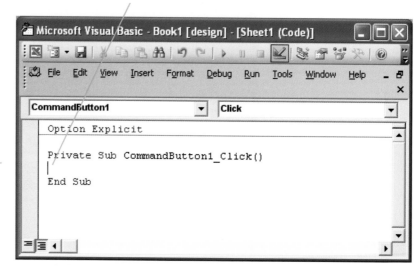

This code module is specific to this particular worksheet. Each worksheet has its own code module in which code can be placed. In this module, you will notice that some code already appears.

`Option Explicit` (if it does appear) will be explained in Chapter 2. It could be considered to invoke spell-checking.

`Private` means that this code can only be referred to in the code module for this particular sheet. It also does not concern us at this stage and could even be omitted if desired.

`CommandButton1` refers to the command button (object) that we placed on the sheet. `Click` is what we are about to do to the command button to run the program.

`Sub` and `End Sub` is a way of indicating a self-contained unit of code. More about subs in Chapter 10.

The VBE will capitalize keywords for you. We can take advantage of this by always typing keywords in lower case. As you press the Enter key, the VBE will capitalize them for you – thereby checking your spelling! For example, type "range" instead of "Range". Words which are not keywords, e.g. "Simple" in this case, of course are not automatically capitalized.

6 Type in the code shown.

```
Private Sub CommandButton1_Click()
Range("A1").Value = "Simple"
End Sub
```

(A drop-down box may appear as you type. This is IntelliSense and is discussed on page 24.) The code above will simply place the word "Simple" into the top left cell of the spreadsheet when we run the program. As we will see, `Value` is a property of the `Range` object and indeed is the default property. Being a default property, it can be omitted, i.e. we could simply have:

```
Range("A1") = "Simple"
```

Extra spaces don't matter (so long as there is at least one between words) when typing your code. The VBE will decide the spacing for you anyway!

7 Go back to the Excel spreadsheet by choosing Excel in the task bar at the bottom of the screen. Alternatively, hold down the Alt key and continue to press Tab until you see the Excel icon – and then release the Alt key. Use these methods to also return to the VBE.

Closing the VBE window by clicking its Close button will not close Excel.

Microsoft Excel - Book1   Microsoft Visual Basic ...

Running your program

Now that you have written the code, it's time to test it.

1 Click the Exit Design Mode button to exit design mode. It should become "deselected".

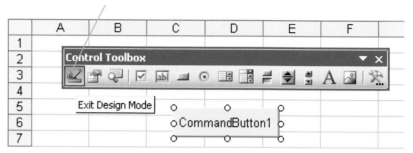

2 The command button has also become "deselected" as shown below. Click on it to run the program.

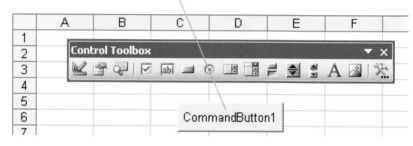

If the code won't run after you have closed and reopened the workbook, it may be that your security setting needs to be changed to Low (from the Excel menu choose Tools, Macro, Security...), but it will not take effect until you close and reopen the workbook. To later guard against macro code from unknown workbooks, set it higher. Users of Excel 97 choose Tools, Options..., General to toggle Macro virus protection.

3 The text appears in cell A1.

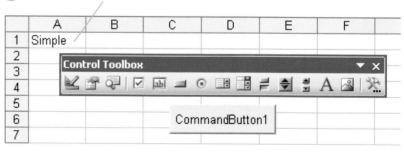

Editing the code

You may have noticed that the command button on the sheet has an "inner rectangle" around it immediately after clicking it – it "has the focus".

1 Return to the VBE by clicking on the View Code button on the Control Toolbox. You will only need to have the Design Mode button depressed if the command button has the focus.

2 Edit the code as shown below.

```
Private Sub CommandButton1_Click()
Range("A2").Value = 2
End Sub
```

A piece of text is known as a string in Visual Basic. If you wish to place a number rather than a string, you don't need the inverted commas.

3 Return to the Excel window. Make sure that the Design Mode button is not depressed. Click on the command button to run the program. Alternatively, you could click on the Run button in the VBE, making sure that your cursor is in the code first.

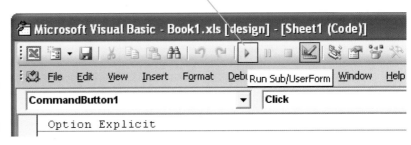

If your text turns red in the VBE after you have typed a line, it indicates that you have made a syntax error. In addition you will receive a message if Auto Syntax Check is turned on (Tools, Options... from the VBE menu). You may prefer to have this option turned off to avoid interruption during certain operations, e.g. cutting and pasting.

4 Return to the Excel window. The number 2 will appear in cell A2.

If your program doesn't run

For example, if you made a spelling mistake, you may get a message like this:

It is worth making a deliberate error like this, even at this stage to see the problems such an error can create.

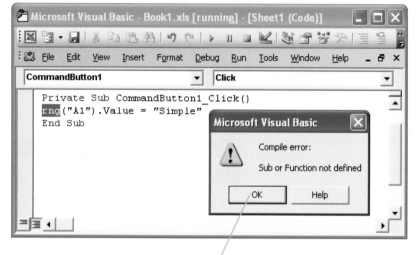

Click OK – but that is not the end of the story!

If you were not to click the Stop button after making such an error, you will find that you are still able to click your command button if you return to the Excel window. It might appear that your program has run, but indeed you will find that it is still stalled in the VBE. This can be a common source of grievance. Alternatively, if you close the VBE window by clicking the close button, you can click OK when warned that "This command will stop the debugger".

You must now click on the Stop button.

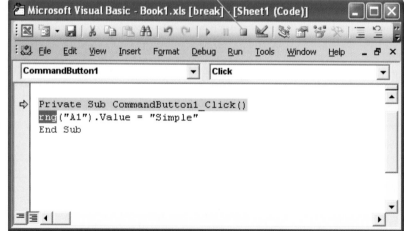

Basic programming techniques

Now that we can write a simple program, we can learn the basic programming techniques to enable us to write useful, practical programs.

Covers

Chapter Two

Variables

After you enter a line containing an illegal variable name in the VBE, the line will turn red.

A variable is a name that we use to store a value. There are a few restrictions on the names that we may choose – for example they cannot start with a number and they cannot contain periods (full-stops), for example x, y1, var1, sumX are legitimate variable names whereas 1x and x.1 are not. Be careful not to use keywords as variable names, e.g. Sub is an illegal name for a variable. Variables are used to store values which you may wish to use later in your program. Variables are categorized depending on the type of data they will contain. A common type is Integer. A variable of Integer type, strictly speaking, can only hold whole number values, e.g.

```
x = 2
```
— Giving a variable a value is known as initializing it

String variable types contain text, e.g.

```
Surname = "Jones"
```

We indicate the type of the variable by using the Dim statement, e.g.

```
Dim x As Integer
Dim Surname As String
```

This is known as *declaring* variables. Different variable types occupy different amounts of space in memory. The Dim statement signals how much memory is going to be required for this particular variable.

We will edit the previous code to include a variable. It will simply place 2 in the top left cell.

```
Option Explicit

Private Sub CommandButton1_Click()
Dim x As Integer
x = 2
Range("A1").Value = x
End Sub
```

Option Explicit, which will be explained later, may or may not be included in your code at this stage

	A	B
1	2	
2		
3		

Swapping Values

Why use variables? Consider this example. We have two integers in two spreadsheet cells as shown below. We wish to write a program to swap them.

	A	B
1	2	
2	3	
3		

First place the two numbers that we wish to swap in the cells as shown

If you were to try the following code it wouldn't work:

```
Range("A1").Value = Range("A2").Value
Range("A2").Value = Range("A1").Value
```

The problem is that the value in A1 gets overwritten and therefore lost. The result would be that both cells would finally contain 3.

We need to be able to save the value in A1 in a variable as follows:

```
Private Sub CommandButton1_Click()
Dim x As Integer
x = Range("A1").Value
Range("A1").Value = Range("A2").Value
Range("A2").Value = x
End Sub
```

The value in A1 is saved in x

The saved value is retrieved

When we run this program by returning to the Excel window and clicking on the command button on the sheet, the values in the cells will be successfully swapped:

	A	B
1	3	
2	2	
3		

Note that if you were to click the command button again, the numbers would again be swapped.

The message box

The message box is a means of displaying data.

The following code will cause a message box to appear when we click the command button on the sheet.

```
Private Sub CommandButton1_Click()
MsgBox "Simple"
End Sub
```

Click OK to dismiss the message box

We can display a combination of text and the value of a variable:

```
Private Sub CommandButton1_Click()
Dim x As Integer
x = 2
MsgBox "The value of x is" & Str(x)
End Sub
```

Whereas the Str() function can actually be omitted (whereby the VBE forces an implicit type conversion from Integer to String), it is not considered good programming practise. Note also that Str() introduces a spurious space on its left, in this case to the left of the 2.

The MsgBox's message (prompt) must be a string (text), hence the Str() function is required to convert an integer to a string, which is then concatenated with the first string using the & operator. More about strings in Chapter 3.

Comments

Comments are text that you can place in the code purely for annotation. Comments play no part in the running of the program. Comments can be useful when later reading through your code to remind you what you did! To make a comment, place an apostrophe at the start of the text. After the line is entered, it should turn green to indicate that it is a comment.

```
Dim x As Integer 'Declare x
'This whole line is a comment
```

Rather than delete a line which you may want to use later, comment it.

If you have many lines that you wish to comment, you can use the Comment Block button which can be placed on your VBE toolbar as follows. From the VBE menu, choose View, Toolbars and then click Customize.... The Customize dialog box should appear as below.

1   Choose the Commands tab.

2   Choose Edit.

3   Drag the Comment Block (and the Uncomment Block) button onto the VBE Toolbar.

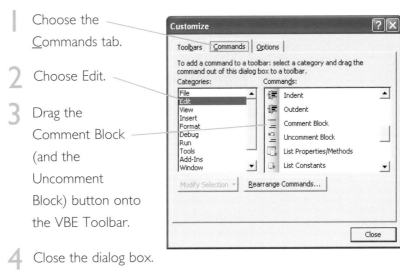

The menu commands of the Excel window and the VBE window are very similar in appearance. Take care to distinguish between them.

4   Close the dialog box.

These buttons should now be visible on your VBE toolbar

Now, in order to comment out a block of text, simply highlight the block and click the Comment Block button. Likewise, in order to uncomment a block, highlight the commented block and click the Uncomment Block button.

Option Explicit

You may have noticed in our previous code examples, that sometimes `Option Explicit` appears and sometimes it doesn't. That's because it is optional! `Option Explicit` at the top of our code module forces us to declare all of our variables, i.e. use `Dim` statements. At the least, `Option Explicit` invokes spell-checking. The example below uses the variable `sales`, but does not use `Option Explicit`. Simply delete/comment it if it is there.

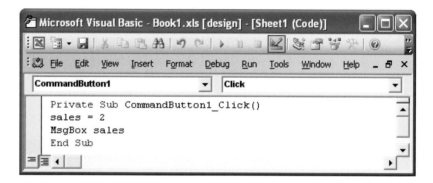

When we run the code by clicking on the command button (first exiting design mode), as we expect, a message box appears displaying the value of 2

In the example below however, the second `sales` variable has been inadvertently misspelled as `sals`. When this program is run, the mistake goes undetected! A message box appears, but with a blank value (see next page), because the misspelled variable `sals` is regarded as *another* legitimate variable without a value!

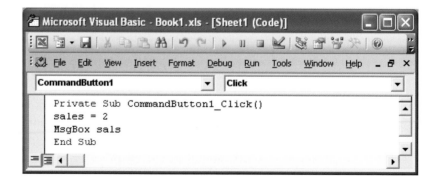

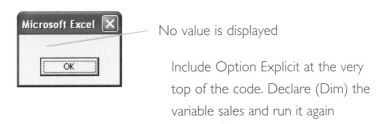

No value is displayed

Include Option Explicit at the very top of the code. Declare (Dim) the variable sales and run it again

Note the strange behavior of the "separating lines", more correctly the Procedure Separators (which can be toggled on/off by first choosing Tools, Options..., Editor), which won't actually appear beneath a line until after the line is entered!

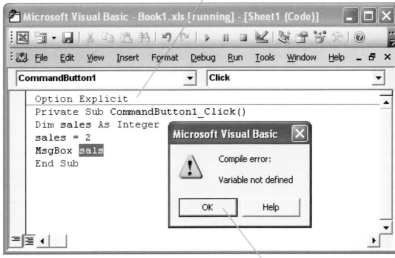

This time the program halts with an error message.
Click OK – and don't forget to click the Stop button!

If you now correct the typo (i.e. change `sals` to `sales`), the program should run as expected, i.e. the message box will correctly display 2.

If using `Option Explicit` may seem a bit unnecessary, even at this early stage, it is a good idea to get used to it now – it will eventually save you time, especially as programs become larger.

Always include Option Explicit at the top of your code – even though it is optional!

`Option Explicit` can be made to appear automatically at the top of your code by checking Require Variable Declaration, after choosing Tools, Options..., Editor from the VBE menu. It will not take effect however, until you open a new workbook. Meanwhile, you can simply type `Option Explicit` in the General Declarations section if it does not already appear.

Other variable types

The `Long` (meaning long integer) variable type is used for large integers up to 2,147,483,647. `Integer` can only take values up to 32,767.

`Single` can cater for decimal values as well as integers.

`Double` (64 bit) is a more accurate version of the 32 bit `Single` type.

`Boolean` can take only the values `True` or `False`.

`Variant` can take any type!

`Date` is used for storing dates. More about `Date` later.

Generally speaking, if you are not sure of the size of variable required, opt for the larger capacity, e.g. use `Long` rather than `Integer`.

The following code segment demonstrates common types:

It is very tempting to declare all variables as Variant. This has disadvantages not only from performance point of view, i.e. your code will run slower, but you should find that errors are easier to isolate if you are more specific about the variable type.

The 1 ("ell") in the default VBA font can be easily mistaken for the VBA 1 (one).

```
Option Explicit
Private Sub CommandButton1_Click()
Dim lg As Long
Dim sg As Single
Dim db As Double
Dim tf As Boolean
Dim vr As Variant
Dim dt As Date
lg = 205
sg = 2.125
db = 2.125
tf = True
vr = 2.6
dt = #1/1/2005#
Range("A1").Value = lg
Range("A2").Value = sg
Range("A3").Value = db
Range("A4").Value = tf
Range("A5").Value = vr
Range("A6").Value = dt
End Sub
```

	A	B
1	205	
2	2.125	
3	2.125	
4	TRUE	
5	2.6	
6	01/01/2005	
7		

It is possible to `Dim` many variables on the same line, e.g.

```
Dim lg As Long, sg As Single, db As Double
```

If we wish to specify a variable as a `Variant` type, we can omit the type qualifier altogether, e.g. instead of `Dim vr As Variant`, we could simply have `Dim vr`, since `Variant` is the default data type.

Take care however when declaring the variables on one line, e.g.

```
Dim x, y, z As Integer
```

will declare x and y as `Variant` and only z as an `Integer`.

An alternative method of declaring variables is to use a type-declaration character. This is a character which is appended to the variable name, e.g. `Dim i As Integer` can be replaced by `Dim i%` and `Dim lg As Long` can be replaced by `Dim lg&`. The use of type-declaration characters however is deprecated, i.e. is to be phased out and eventually not supported, and is only mentioned here in case it is encountered.

It is good programming practise to ensure that all variable declarations are placed at the very start of the code.

Unfortunately, with Excel VBA, it is not yet possible to declare and initialize a variable in one statement, e.g.

```
Dim s As Single = 22.1
```

is not yet possible.

IntelliSense

If IntelliSense does not appear, from the VBE menu, choose Tools, Options..., and check Auto List Members.

IntelliSense can be made to appear at any time by pressing Ctrl+Spacebar.

You have probably by now, noticed a drop-down box which sometimes appears as you type. This is IntelliSense.

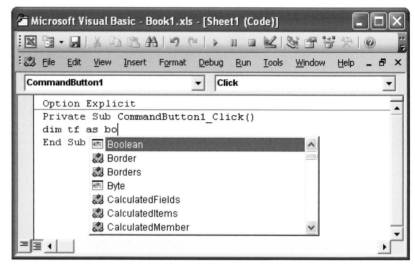

IntelliSense is a feature of the VBE which allows you to easily complete your line of code.

Note that as a space is typed, as in the above example after the "as", IntelliSense appears. As further letters are typed, the IntelliSense suggestions become more specific. To accept the suggestion, either implicitly accept the suggestion by continuing to type the remainder of the line, or double-click on the suggestion. If the Enter key is pressed to accept the highlighted suggestion, a new line will be also started.

To accept the IntelliSense suggestion without starting a new line, press the Tab key.

You will also notice that IntelliSense will sometimes even make a suggestion for the *value* of a variable. For example, in our case, as shown below, when "tf =" is typed, True or False is suggested, but only if you are declaring your variables using Dim etc.

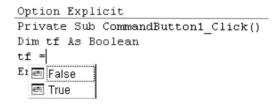

Help

To get Help, you can sometimes simply place the cursor in a word and press F1.

Excel VBA Help is not installed by default in a standard installation of Microsoft Office. You may need to run the Office setup program again and choose the option to install it.

Help can also be accessed by choosing Help from the VBE menu and clicking Microsoft Visual Basic Help.

Excel VBA has a very comprehensive built-in reference. The most reliable way to get Help is the easiest! Simply highlight the word (you could double-click on the word) for which you want Help, and then press the F1 key. For example, highlight the keyword `Boolean` as shown below and then press the F1 key.

```
Option Explicit
Private Sub CommandButton1_Click()
Dim tf As Boolean

End Sub
```

The Help dialog box appears as shown below.

Try the See Also and then choose Data Type Summary where you should find data types that we have not yet discussed

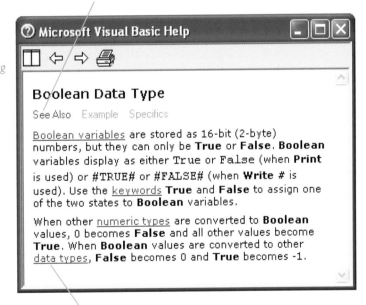

Boolean Data Type

See Also   Example   Specifics

Boolean variables are stored as 16-bit (2-byte) numbers, but they can only be **True** or **False**. Boolean variables display as either True or False (when **Print** is used) or #TRUE# or #FALSE# (when **Write #** is used). Use the keywords **True** and **False** to assign one of the two states to **Boolean** variables.

When other numeric types are converted to **Boolean** values, 0 becomes **False** and all other values become **True**. When **Boolean** values are converted to other data types, **False** becomes 0 and **True** becomes -1.

Try the hyperlinks for some extremely useful definitions. The hyperlinks change color after being "visited"

Arithmetic operations

You are most probably already familiar with Excel formulas.

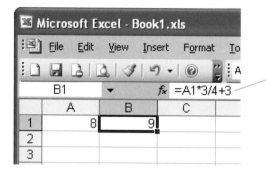

This formula of course will multiply the contents of A1 by 3, divide by 4 and then add 3 to the result giving 9

The same operator symbols are used in VBA. We could carry out the above operation in VBA as follows:

Use the Single or Double data type when the result could be a decimal number.

```
Private Sub CommandButton1_Click()
Dim x As Single
x = Range("a1").Value
Range("B1").Value = x * 3 / 4 + 3
End Sub
```

This line should cause 9 to be placed in cell B1

Try the exponentiation operator – replace the corresponding line above with:

```
Range("B1").Value = x ^ 2
```

in which case the value of x is raised to the power of 2, i.e. in this case, 8 is squared to give 64 and placed in B1.

As in Excel itself, parentheses ensure priority as shown below:

```
Private Sub CommandButton1_Click()
Dim x As Single
x = 8
Range("A1").Value = 16 / x - 1
Range("A2").Value = 18 /(x + 1)
End Sub
```

16 is divided by 8, and then 1 is subtracted to give 1

18 is divided by the sum of 8 plus 1 to give 2

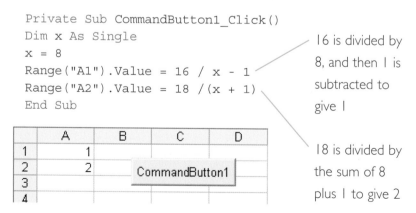

Branching and looping

Now that we can write a simple program, we can proceed to learn the basic programming techniques which will enable us to write useful, practical programs.

Covers

Chapter Three

The For...Next loop

The For...Next loop is one of the most useful program constructs. We usually first declare an Integer counter variable which will get automatically incremented as control is transferred cyclically from the last line of the loop to the first. The For...Next keyword pair serve to enclose the code.

This code will simply cause a message box to appear three times after the command button is clicked to run the program.

Use the Tab key to indent a line of code in order to improve legibility.

```
Private Sub CommandButton1_Click()
Dim i As Integer
    For i = 1 To 3
    MsgBox "Simple"
    Next i
End Sub
```

After reaching Next, control is transferred back to For.

The message box will appear (and need to be dismissed) three times.

The For keyword signals the start of the loop. The value of i is initially 1. Program control continues down, line by line – the message box is displayed – until the Next keyword is reached. Program control then automatically returns to the For above.

The value of i is then incremented to 2. This process continues until i becomes 3 – control is no longer transferred back to the For but continues down to the statement after the Next – the End Sub whereupon the program terminates.

Change the code to that shown below so that the message box will now display 1, 2 and 3 respectively.

```
Private Sub CommandButton1_Click()
Dim i As Integer
    For i = 1 To 3
    MsgBox Str(i)
    Next i
End Sub
```

Using Cells

`Cells` is an alternative to `Range`. It is used to refer to a particular spreadsheet cell using indices. `Cells(1,2)` for example would refer to the cell of row 1 and column 2 using the indices 1 and the 2. The equivalent, using the `Range` notation would be `Range("B1")`, so to place a 3 in cell B1 we would use:

```
Private Sub CommandButton1_Click()
Cells(1, 2).Value = 3
End Sub
```

	A	B	C	D
1		3		
2				
3				
4		CommandButton1		
5				

The advantage of using the `Cells` notation is that it can be used with variable indices, which is particularly useful for looping as we shall now see. This program simply places the number 10 in the first five cells of the first column.

```
Private Sub CommandButton1_Click()
Dim i As Integer
  For i = 1 To 5
  Cells(i, 1).Value = 10
  Next i
End Sub
```

	A	B	C	D
1	10			
2	10			
3	10			
4	10	CommandButton1		
5	10			

The `Cells` notation can also be used to *get* values from a cell. To read the value in cell B1 into a variable x we would use:

```
x = Cells(1,2).Value
```

The debugger

The debugger tool assists with finding errors. It can be used to step through the code one line at a time. This is useful for instructional purposes – the program can be run in slow motion!

1 View the previous program in the VBE and place the cursor at the start.

Instead of pressing the F8 key, from the VBE menu you can choose Debug, Step Into.

```
Option Explicit
Private Sub CommandButton1_Click()
Dim i As Integer
For i = 1 To 5
Cells(i, 1).Value = 10
Next i
End Sub
```

2 Press the F8 key to single step through the code.

If the Excel window is arranged alongside the VBE window, the values can be seen being placed simultaneously on the sheet – one by one – as you single step through the code!

The yellow bar shows the current line

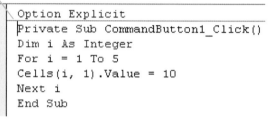

```
Option Explicit
⇨ Private Sub CommandButton1_Click()
Dim i As Integer
For i = 1 To 5
Cells(i, 1).Value = 10
Next i
End Sub
```

3 Continue to press F8 to single step. Note that it doesn't seem to "land" on the For statement as it cycles around the loop.

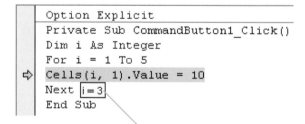

```
Option Explicit
Private Sub CommandButton1_Click()
Dim i As Integer
For i = 1 To 5
⇨ Cells(i, 1).Value = 10
Next i=3
End Sub
```

To enable this "little yellow box" (more correctly the Data Tips window), make sure that Auto Data Tips is checked – choose Tools, Options..., Editor from the VBE menu.

If you very carefully place your cursor on a variable as you debug, the value of the variable will appear in a small yellow box

4 If you wish to stop single stepping, click the Stop button or click the triangular Continue button to continue running.

Breakpoints

The program can be made to halt temporarily at a particular line by using a breakpoint.

1   Click on the left margin of the VBE at the point where you would like to set a breakpoint. A brown/maroon dot appears.

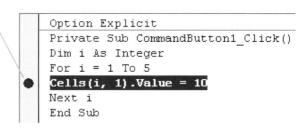

2   Run the program by clicking the command button on the spreadsheet, or by clicking the Run button from the VBE, making sure that the cursor is within the code. The program will halt at the breakpoint.

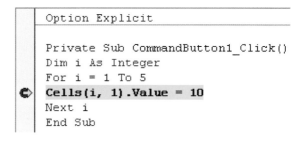

The F5 key can also be used from the VBE to run the program. Make sure that the cursor is at the start of the code.

3   By holding the cursor steady on a variable, we can inspect the value of the variable as we saw previously. Single step by pressing the F8 key or continue to click the Continue (Run) button to run (loop) to the breakpoint. If you wish to stop the program, click the Reset (Stop) button.

4   To remove the breakpoint, simply click on it. To clear all breakpoints, from the VBE menu choose Debug, Clear All Breakpoints.

The Immediate window

The Immediate window is used to display output and accept input whilst debugging. It can be used to display values of variables as the program single steps. To display the Immediate window, from the VBE menu choose View, Immediate Window.

`Debug.Print` is used in the code to send output from your program to the Immediate window. Include `Debug.Print i` in the code of the previous example as shown below, and single step (continue pressing F8). In this case, the value of the counter will be printed to the Immediate window for each loop.

```
Private Sub CommandButton1_Click()
Dim i As Integer
   For i = 1 To 5
   Cells(i, 1).Value = 10
   Debug.Print i
   Next i
End Sub
```

Debug.Print i will cause the value of i to be output to the Immediate window as the program loops

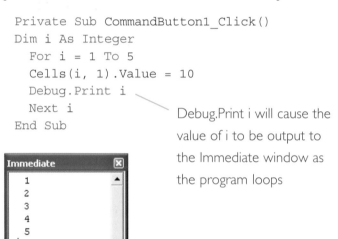

Whilst debugging, you can type directly into the Immediate window while the program is temporarily halted (break mode). Typing print i will cause the value of i to appear.

If you wish to repeat a command whilst in the Immediate window, simply place your cursor at the end of the command and press the Enter key.

Print i can be abbreviated to ?i.

If...Then

Another extremely important statement pair is the `If...Then` pair. An action is either performed or not performed, depending on whether a condition is satisfied.

```
Private Sub CommandButton1_Click()
Dim i As Integer
i = 2
    If i = 2 Then Cells(1, 1).Value = "yes"
End Sub
```

Since the condition is fulfilled, "yes" is placed in cell A1

	A	B	C	D
1	yes			
2				
3		CommandButton1		
4				
5				

Change `i = 2` to `i = 3`. The condition `i = 2` now of course is false. When the program runs, nothing happens. Make sure that you delete the "yes" in the spreadsheet before you run the program else you won't see that nothing has happened!

We have just seen how the `If...Then` construction was placed on one line. It can be "split" by placing the conditional code in an `If....End If` block as shown below.

When run, this code will perform exactly as the previous code.

```
Option Explicit
Private Sub CommandButton1_Click()
Dim i As Integer
i = 2
    If i = 2 Then
    Cells(1, 1).Value = "yes"
    End If
End Sub
```

The If and End If serve to enclose the conditional code

No matter what construction is used, the If and Then are always on the same line.

The advantage of this construction is that more than one statement can be executed if the condition is satisfied, as we will now see.

```
Private Sub CommandButton1_Click()
Dim i As Integer
i = 2
   If i = 2 Then
   Cells(1, 1).Value = "yes"
   Cells(1, 2).Value = "of course"
   End If
End Sub
```

The If and End If now enclose more than one statement

The result of running the previous code is that text appears in two cells

	A	B	C	D	E
1	yes	of course			
2					
3		CommandButton1			
4					
5					

Else

Before proceeding, clear the cells A1 and B1.
Else is used with If...Then to cater for the alternative.

```
Private Sub CommandButton1_Click()
Dim i As Integer
i = 1
   If i = 2 Then
   Cells(1, 1).Value = "yes"
   Cells(1, 2).Value = "of course"
   Else
   Cells(2, 1).Value = "sorry"
   End If
End Sub
```

Since the condition is not satisfied, only the Else section of the code is performed

	A	B	C	D	E
1					
2	sorry				
3		CommandButton1			
4					
5					

Logical operators

The most common logical operators are And, Or and Not.

When each of the three simple programs below is run, the result will be the same – "yes" will be placed in the top left cell of the spreadsheet in each case.

And

To put two statements on one line, place a colon (:) in between.

```
Private Sub CommandButton1_Click()
Dim i As Integer, j As Integer
i = 1 : j = 2
If i = 1 And j = 2 Then Cells(1,1) = "yes"
End Sub
```

Both conditions
must be true

Or

```
Private Sub CommandButton1_Click()
Dim i As Integer, j As Integer
i = 1 : j = 3
If i = 1 Or j = 2 Then Cells(1,1) = "yes"
End Sub
```

Either condition
is sufficient

Not

```
Private Sub CommandButton1_Click()
Dim i As Integer
i = 1
If Not i = 2 Then Cells(1,1) = "yes"
End Sub
```

Any value for i other than 2 will
result in the condition being satisfied

	A	B	C	D	E
1	yes				
2					
3		CommandButton1			
4					
5					

Do...Loops

Do and Loop also occur in pairs and serve to enclose code which "repeats". The program below will perform exactly as the For...Next example we met previously. It will place five 10's in the first column of the sheet. Whereas the For...Next loop will increment the counter for us automatically, when using the Do...Loop we must increment it explicitly.

```
Private Sub CommandButton1_Click()
Dim i As Integer
i = 0
Do
i = i + 1
Cells(i, 1) = 10
Loop Until i = 5
End Sub
```

The statement i = i + 1 means "take the present value of i and add 1 to it"

For values of i less than 5, control is transferred back to the Do. When i finally becomes 5, the loop terminates

When we click on the Command Button on the sheet, five 10's are placed in the first column

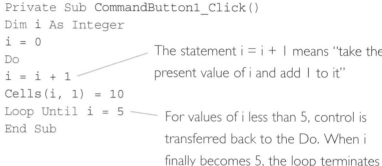

	A	B	C	D
1	10			
2	10			
3	10	CommandButton1		
4	10			
5	10			
6				

The following is a variation of the above. Five 10's will be placed in the first column as shown above.

```
Private Sub CommandButton1_Click()
Dim i As Integer
i = 0
Do Until i = 5
i = i + 1
Cells(i, 1) = 10
Loop
End Sub
```

The only difference is that the condition is tested at the start of the loop. After i becomes 5 inside the loop and then Loop is encountered, control is transferred back to the Do Until whereupon the loop terminates

Instead of Do...Until, we may use Do...While.

Again the effect of this code will be identical.

```
Private Sub CommandButton1_Click()
Dim i As Integer
i = 0
Do While i < 5
i = i + 1
Cells(i, 1) = 10
Loop
End Sub
```

i < 5 allows the loop to be entered while i is less than 5, but when i becomes 5 inside the loop, Loop transfers control back to the Do While and the loop terminates

	A	B	C	D
1	10			
2	10			
3	10	CommandButton1		
4	10			
5	10			
6				

As you can see, the differences between loops using Do...Loop is quite subtle – familiarity with one would suffice at this stage.

The condition after the Do or the Loop, e.g. i < 5, evaluates to either True or False. If we were to run something like this...

```
Do While False

Loop
```

Since the condition is False, the program doesn't loop at all

...nothing would happen, it wouldn't loop at all. Whereas the following code would loop forever. Don't try this!

```
Do While True

Loop
```

Since the condition is True, the program would loop continuously

To halt a continuous loop, press Ctrl+Break on the keyboard.

In general, a For...Next loop is used when the number of loops required is quite definite, whereas the other loops, e.g. Do...While are used when a variable, which is not necessarily the loop counter, meets a condition inside the loop.

Select Case

Select Case is like a multiple If statement. The option chosen will depend on the value of a variable.

```
Private Sub CommandButton1_Click()
Dim x As Integer
x = 7
    Select Case x
    Case 5
    MsgBox "Five"
    Case 7
    MsgBox "Seven"
    End Select
End Sub
```

The value of the variable x will determine which Case is selected

Since the value of x is 7, this section of the code (only) will be executed

End Select always accompanies Select Case

As a result of running the program, the message box will appear as below.

From the VBE, take a look at the Help for Select Case.

The most convenient way to get Help is to select the words (e.g. Select Case) in the VBE and press F1.

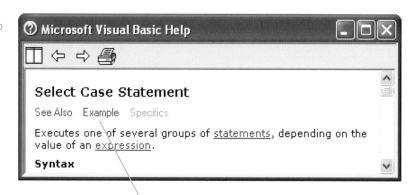

When using this particular Help Example, make sure that the Immediate window is open. From the VBE choose View, Immediate Window or Ctrl+G to see the result of the Debug.Print statement.

The Help Example is particularly useful. Copy and paste it into the CommandButton procedure. Note in the example how the option chosen can depend on a range of values rather than a single value. Note also the use of the comparison operators Is < and Is >

A practical example

A salesman receives a commission which increases with his sales.

For sales of less than 1000 dollars he receives 5 %.
Between 1000 and 2000 dollars (inclusive) he receives 10 %.
For greater than 2000 dollars he receives 15 %.

We want to enter the sales value into cell A2, and then click
the command button for his commission to appear in B2

	A	B	C	D	E
1	Sales	Commision			
2	1500	150	CommandButton1		
3					
4					

```
Private Sub CommandButton1_Click()
Dim sales As Single, comm As Single
sales = Cells(2, 1).Value
Select Case sales
   Case Is < 1000
         comm = 0.05
   Case 1000 To 2000
         comm = 0.1
   Case Is > 2000
         comm = 0.15
End Select
Cells(2, 2).Value = sales * comm
End Sub
```

The sales value is obtained from the cell A2

The commission percentage is determined by the value of sales

The total amount of commission that he receives will be calculated and appear in cell B2

Program development

We wish to write a program which will indicate by means of a message box, the number of occurrences of a particular number, in this case, the number of occurrences of 12, as shown below. First place eight numbers (including some 12's) in the first column of a sheet as shown.

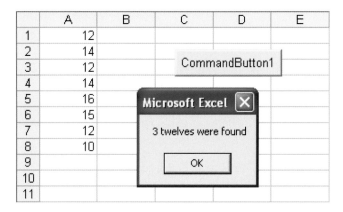

Rather than write the complete program to do this in one attempt, we will write and test small sections, and finally piece them together – step by step.

Write some code to output all of the eight values in column A one at a time.

```
Private Sub CommandButton1_Click()
Dim i As Integer
  For i = 1 To 8
  MsgBox Cells(i,1).Value
  Next i
End Sub
```

The row value of Cells(i , 1) is increased by 1 each time it loops

Eight message boxes should appear with the respective values

2 Have the message box appear only if the value in the cell is 12. Use an If. In our example, the message box displaying 12 should appear 3 times.

```
Private Sub CommandButton1_Click()
Dim i As Integer
  For i = 1 To 8
    If Cells(i,1).Value = 12 Then
    Msgbox Cells(i,1).Value
    End If
  Next i
End Sub
```

3 Use a counter (c in this case), and increment it each time that a 12 is encountered. Finally, include a MsgBox statement after the loop has ended to report the value of this counter.

```
Private Sub CommandButton1_Click()
Dim i As Integer, c As Integer
c = 0
  For i = 1 To 8
    If Cells(i,1).Value = 12 Then
    c = c + 1
    End If
  Next i
MsgBox Str(c) & " twelve/s found"
End Sub
```

To indent a block of code to make it more legible, highlight the block that you wish to indent and press the Tab key. To "un-indent", more correctly to outdent it, highlight it and press Shift+Tab.

4 When the program is run, we should get a message box indicating the number of 12's found.

Using a flag

What if we wished to know not *how many* 12's there are, but whether there *is* a 12 in a list of numbers? We need to indicate or flag that a 12 was found. It is usual to declare a flag as a `Boolean` type and initially set it to `False`. The default value of a `Boolean` type is `False`, but it is always good practise to initialize variables explicitly. If a 12 is found, we could use an `If` statement to set the flag variable to `True` and after exiting the loop, use a message box to display the state of the flag as shown.

```
Private Sub CommandButton1_Click()
Dim i As Integer, fl As Boolean
fl = False
  For i = 1 To 8
    If Cells(i, 1).Value = 12 Then fl = True
  Next i
  If fl = True Then
  MsgBox "Found a 12"
  Else
  MsgBox "12 not found"
  End If
End Sub
```

If a 12 is found, then the flag is set to True

You could try removing all of the 12's from the values in column A to test the Else condition

For the sake of code efficiency, the `For...Next` loop in the above program could be modified to include an `Exit For` as shown below, so that when *one* 12 is found, the `For...Next` could be terminated and the flag would not repeatedly be set to `True` each time *another* 12 was found. If the debugger were used to single step, you would see an exit from the `For...Next` as soon as the first 12 was found.

```
For i = 1 To 8
  If Cells(i, 1).Value = 12 Then
  fl = True
  Exit For
  End If
Next i
```

Note that we need to use an If...End If because there is more than one statement to be executed if a 12 is encountered

Adding flexibility

So far, we have written a program that searches for the number of 12's. The 12 is built into the program. What if we wished to search for 14 or a 15? How should we let our program know what number to look for? We will enter it into a cell (C1 in our case) on the sheet itself, and then click the command button to find whether this number is in our set of numbers.

```
Private Sub CommandButton1_Click()
Dim i As Integer, fl As Boolean, x As Variant
x = Cells(1, 3).Value
fl = False

For i = 1 To 8
If Cells(i, 1).Value = x Then
fl = True
Exit For
End If
Next i

If fl = True Then
MsgBox "Found a " & x
Else
MsgBox x & " not found"
End If
End Sub
```

The number that we wish to search for is input from cell C1

If the number is found, the flag is set to True and the loop is exited

The message box will also remind us of the number that we are looking for

Sometimes an error message will appear warning that you have a "Next without For", where in reality it's an End If that's missing.

Save this code for a following exercise. A convenient way to do this is to comment it and perhaps drag it out of the CommandButton procedure.

The number that we are to look for is placed in cell C1. Fully test the code by using a number which is not in column A

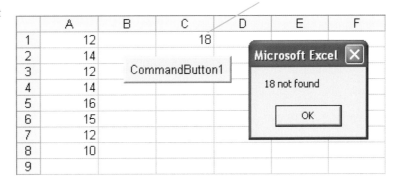

Loops inside loops

We wish to write a program which will iterate through this table of values and display them one at a time using a message box. First, use the code below to iterate across the top row only.

	A	B	C	D	E
1	12	10	16	32	
2	22	15	24	21	
3	12	23	22	13	
4					

Reduce and rearrange both the Excel window and the VBE window to be able to see your code in action.

```
Private Sub CommandButton1_Click()
Dim j As Integer
    For j = 1 To 4
    Cells(1, j).Select
    MsgBox Cells(1, j).Value
    Next j
End Sub
```

The Select statement is only included so that the cell will appear selected each time the message box appears

So far, we have iterated through the first row only. In order to move *down* one row at a time in order to iterate through the next two rows, we need another loop. The counter of this outer loop (i), will need to increment from 1 to 3, thereby incrementing the row number.

```
Private Sub CommandButton1_Click()
Dim i As Integer,j As Integer
For i = 1 To 3
    For j = 1 To 4
    Cells(i, j).Select
    MsgBox Cells(i, j).Value
    Next j
Next i
End Sub
```

For each of the 3 values of i (the row number), the inner loop cycles 4 times

Watch the selection move across and then down

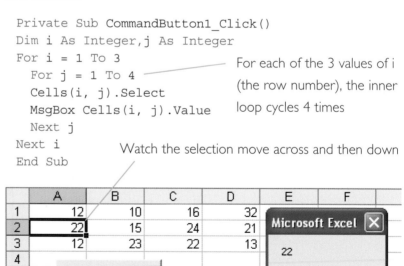

A number search

In a previous example, we searched through a list of numbers in column A to find a number which was read in from a particular spreadsheet cell. What if we wanted to find a series of such numbers?

In this example, we want to search for each of the three numbers in column C, one at a time, to see if they exist in the list of eight numbers in column A. We need a loop inside a loop.

	A	B	C	D
1	12		12	
2	14		10	
3	12		16	
4	14			
5	16			
6	15			
7	12			
8	10			
9				

We want to determine whether these numbers are in column A. Of course they all are presently!

When your statement won't fit onto one line, use the special line continuation character. Type a space followed by an underscore and then press the Enter key. Don't forget the space!

```
Private Sub CommandButton1_Click()
Dim i As Integer, fl As Boolean, _
x As Variant, j As Integer
For j = 1 To 3
fl = False
x = Cells(j, 3).Value
  For i = 1 To 8
    If Cells(i, 1).Value = x Then
    fl = True
    Exit For
    End If
  Next i
  If fl = True Then
  MsgBox "Found a " & x
  Else
  MsgBox x & " not found"
  End If
Next j
End Sub
```

The outer loop iterates through the 3 values in column C

If the value is found in column A, set the flag = True and exit the inner loop

Always test code under all conditions. In this example include a number in column C (e.g. 18) which is not in column A.

Three such message boxes will appear in our example

Microsoft Excel [X]
Found a 16
OK

A program to delete blank cells

A multiple selection can also be made holding down the Ctrl key whilst selecting.

We are able to delete blank cells from Excel, but the method has a shortcoming: if we were to first select the blank cells by selecting the whole range and choosing Edit, Go To..., Special..., Blanks and then from the Excel menu, delete them using Edit, Delete..., Shift cells up, all cells beneath the selection would be moved up as well! How can we avoid also moving these cells up? VBA to the rescue! Once again, rather than write the program to do this in one attempt, we will develop our program in a step by step manner, testing the techniques required as we go.

Whilst testing and developing, it's a good idea to have a reserve set of values on the same sheet which can be quickly copied across if the originals are erroneously altered by your code.

	A	B	C	D	E	F
1	12					
2						
3				CommandButton1		
4	14					
5						
6	16					
7	20					
8	22					
9						

For the moment, let's make the requirement a bit simpler. Say that we are now required only to move all of the cells to the *right* which are non-blank, as shown below.

	A	B	C	D	E	F
1	12	12				
2						
3				CommandButton1		
4	14	14				
5						
6	16	16				
7	20	20				
8	22	22				
9						

The following code should perform that task.

```
Private Sub CommandButton1_Click()
Dim i As Integer
For i = 1 To 8
   If Cells(i, 1) <> "" Then
   Cells(i, 2).Value = Cells(i, 1).Value
   End If
Next i
End Sub
```

"" indicates a blank (empty cell)

<> means "not equal to"

The contents of the cell in column 1 is copied to the corresponding cell (on the same row) in column 2

Say that we now require the cells in the second column to be "bunched up"– with no spaces, as shown below.

	A	B	C	D	E	F
1	12	12				
2		14				
3		16		CommandButton1		
4	14	20				
5		22				
6	16					
7	20					
8	22					
9						

To achieve this, we need a counter which will keep track of the number of occupied cells in the second column. We will use c as this counter and increment c each time that a cell is copied across – each time that a non-blank is found.

```
Private Sub CommandButton1_Click()
Dim i As Integer, c As Integer
c = 0
For i = 1 To 8
   If Cells(i, 1) <> "" Then
   c = c + 1
   Cells(c, 2).Value = Cells(i, 1).Value
   End If
Next i
End Sub
```

The variable c keeps track of the next available row in column B

We will now apply this same counter technique to the values in the first column in order to "bunch them up". So change

```
Cells(c, 2).Value = Cells(i, 1).Value to:
```

```
Cells(c, 1).Value = Cells(i, 1).Value
```

Having moved the contents of a non-blank cell up, we then need to delete the cell contents by including:

```
Cells(i, 1).Value = ""
```

Our code should now look like this:

```
Private Sub CommandButton1_Click()
Dim i As Integer, c As Integer
c = 0
For i = 1 To 8
  If Cells(i, 1) <> "" Then
  c = c + 1
  Cells(c, 1).Value = Cells(i, 1).Value
  Cells(i, 1).Value = ""
  End If
Next i
End Sub
```

The intention is to delete the cell contents after it has been copied up

Unfortunately it doesn't work. Any non-blank cells above the first blank (in this case the 12) are being erroneously deleted. We need to find a way to prevent these deletions. Try single stepping, and carefully take note of the values of i and c.

	A
1	12
2	
3	
4	14
5	
6	16
7	20
8	22
9	

1 When i has the value of 1, a non-blank is encountered and therefore c is increased to 1. We don't wish this 12 to be deleted.

2 As blanks are encountered, i increases, but c remains fixed at 1 in this case.

3 When the next non-blank is encountered, i = 4 of course, but c has only been increased to 2. 14 is to be deleted.

We want deletions to occur only if a cell has been moved up – in which case, the value of c will be less than the value of i as we have just seen. We therefore need to add this condition in the form of an If statement:

```
If c < i Then...
```

When the necessary If is included, the final version should look like this:

```
Private Sub CommandButton1_Click()
Dim i As Integer, c As Integer
c = 0
For i = 1 To 8
  If Cells(i, 1).Value <> "" Then
  c = c + 1
    If c < i Then
    Cells(c, 1).Value = Cells(i, 1).Value
    Cells(i, 1).Value = ""
    End If
  End If
Next i
End Sub
```

If a blank has yet to be encountered c will be less than i

Now the cell will be cleared only if the cell's content has been moved up

Just because a cell appears to have no contents, it may not be blank – it could have a space! You may like to use the Trim function which removes any leading or trailing spaces from a string to make sure, e.g. Trim(Cells(i,1).Value).

The blanks have been removed. You may wish to also check that no cells beneath the range have been moved up!

String handling

We previously mentioned that a piece of text is known as a string in VBA (and many other languages as well). We can use special functions to join (concatenate) them, split them, search for one string inside another, etc.

We have seen how to declare and initialize `String` types:

```
Dim st1 As String, st2 As String

st1 = "house" : st2 = "boat"
```

Concatenation

To join two strings, use the `&` operator.

```
Cells(1, 1) = st1 & st2
```

"house" and "boat" are concatenated to give "houseboat"

Place these lines of code into a command button procedure. Run the following lines of code as well.

Left

`Left` extracts the leftmost characters from a string, e.g.

```
Cells(2, 1) = Left(st1, 2)
```

The 2 leftmost characters of "house", i.e. "ho" are extracted

Right

`Right` extracts the rightmost characters from a string, e.g.

```
Cells(3, 1) = Right(st1, 2)
```

The 2 rightmost characters of "house", i.e. "se" are extracted

Instr

`Instr` finds the position of a substring in a string, e.g.

```
Cells(4, 1) = InStr(st1, "us")
```

The position of the string "us" inside the string "house" is found – at position 3

Mid

Mid extracts a substring, e.g.

```
Cells(5, 1) = Mid(st1, 3, 2)
```

The substring of the string "house", starting at position 3 and of length 2, i.e. "us" is extracted

Len

Len simply finds the length of the string, i.e. the number of characters, e.g.

```
Cells(6, 1) = Len(st1)
```

The length of the string "house" is determined, i.e. 5 characters.

The results of all of these lines of code is shown below:

	A
1	houseboat
2	ho
3	se
4	3
5	us
6	5
7	

"house" & "boat"

Left("house",2)

Right("house",2)

Instr("house","us")

Mid("house", 3, 2)

Len("house")

When using the Mid function, if we don't specify the last number, the substring extracted will be the rest of the string to the right, from the position specified, e.g. if instead of Mid("house", 3, 2) which produced "us", we used Mid("house", 3) then "use" would result. When extracting characters to the right from a string, the Mid function is surprisingly more useful than Right, since it is usually more convenient to specify the *starting position* for string extraction, rather than the *number* of characters to the right to be extracted.

See Help for more information about other interesting string-related functions e.g. Trim, CStr, Val, etc.

To rearrange a string

We are given a person's full name, e.g. Jack Robinson. We wish to convert this to the format Robinson,Jack i.e. the surname followed by a comma (no space), followed by the Christian name. We require this technique to work for any Christian name-surname pair. First we must extract the Christian name.

Before that, we need to find the position of the space. We can then extract all of the characters to the left of this position (the Christian name). We then need to extract all of the characters to the right of this position (the surname). Finally we can concatenate the surname with the Christian name (in that order), not forgetting to put a comma in between.

Place the full name to be processed in cell A1 and run this code.

```
Private Sub CommandButton1_Click()
Dim fullName As String, pos As Integer, _
cn As String, sn As String, newName As String
fullName = Cells(1,1).Value    'name is in cell A1
pos = InStr(fullName, " ")     'position of space
cn = Left(fullName, pos - 1)   'Christian name
sn = Mid(fullName, pos + 1)    'surname
newName = sn & "," & cn
Cells(1, 2) = newName          'B1 holds new name
End Sub
```

Test it by trying a different full name in cell A1.

This technique could be employed for example to loop through a set of full names in the column of a spreadsheet and place the names with the modified format in the next column to the right as shown below:

	A	B	C
1	Jack Robinson	Robinson,Jack	
2	Joe DeMaggio	DeMaggio,Joe	
3	James Last	Last,James	
4			

Objects and the Excel Object Model

We often hear how computer programming has become "object-oriented" – and indeed it has. Whereas Excel VBA is not a truly object-oriented language, we learn in this chapter what an object is in its simplest form, and how objects are categorized in the Microsoft Excel Object Model.

Covers

Chapter Four

Properties and methods

An object has properties and methods. We have already met an example of an object – the `Range` object. Properties are something which an object *has*, whereas methods *do* something. As we will now see, properties and methods are associated with an object by means of the dot operator (period/full-stop).

Properties

An object can have more than one property. Properties have values. They are usually preceded by the dot operator and then the object, thereby associating them with that particular object, as we have seen with `Range("A1").Value` for example. Recall that `Value` is the default property and could therefore be omitted.

The `Count` property, when applied to `Range` objects indicates the number of cells in the corresponding range. For example:

```
Private Sub CommandButton1_Click()
MsgBox Range("A1:A3").Count
End Sub
```

The number of
cells in the range
A1:A3 is 3

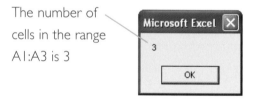

Methods

Methods usually perform some operation on the object with which they are associated. We have already briefly mentioned the `Select` method, which we used to select a single cell. We can even use the `Select` method to select more than one cell.

If this code is run, a range of cells A1:C2 will be selected as shown on the next page.

```
Private Sub CommandButton1_Click()
Range("A1:C2").Select
End Sub
```

	A	B	C	D
1				
2				
3				
4		CommandButton1		
5				

The `ClearContents` method will clear the contents of a cell. It is the VBA equivalent of the Excel Edit, Clear, Contents command. For example, the following code will clear the contents of cell A1.

```
Private Sub CommandButton1_Click()
Range("A1").ClearContents
End Sub
```

The `ClearContents` method of clearing a cell as above, is an alternative to the more primitive `Range("A1").Value = ""` that we saw previously.

Recall that the IntelliSense drop-down will appear (in this case after the period is typed) to show us a list of suggestions. The suggestions are either methods (the "flying green bricks") or properties (the "pointing fingers").

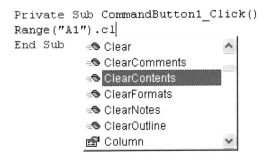

Object hierarchy

Objects can belong to other objects. The dot operator is used to associate objects.

For example, the `Font` object belongs to the `Range` object. Being an object, `Font` has properties, e.g. the `Bold` property. The `Font` object is a little exceptional however, as it has no methods.

For example, to make the contents of cell A1 bold, we could use:

```
Range("A1").Font.Bold = True
```

Object or property?

If we consult the VBA Help for `Font`, you will find a brief description of `Font` as a *property*, and `Font` as an *object* where you will find a comprehensive list of the `Font` object's properties. `Font`, *as it appears in code* is a property. It is a property which "produces" a `Font` object. We say that the `Font` property *returns* a `Font` object.

The distinction between the `Font` property and the `Font` object is somewhat academic. For all intents and purposes, it is the properties and methods of the corresponding objects that we wish to access, so to that end we ought to navigate in the VBA Help to the respective *objects* – in this case the `Font` object and ascertain its properties (and usually methods) – for example, the `Bold` property.

It is no less confusing to hear that `Range` as it appears in code as above, is also a property. It is a property which returns a `Range` object.

Instead of the `Range`, of course we could use `Cells`.

```
Cells(1,1).Font.Bold = True
```

`Cells`, as it appears in code, as above, is also a property! If you search Help for `Cells`, you will see that it is described as a property (there is no `Cells` object!). `Cells` is a property which *returns* a `Range` object (there are many other properties which return a `Range` object). In practical terms, this simply means that in order to ascertain the properties and methods of `Cells`, we need to locate the properties and methods of the `Range` object.

When seeking VBA Help it is probably even worth temporarily typing the word into the VBE, highlighting it, and then pressing the F1 key, rather than using the Help dialog box.

Ambiguity confuses! Range is an object, which as we will see, is returned by many properties, e.g. Cells, ActiveCell, Selection, Columns, Rows and...Range!

You may even see Range described as a collection (see later), which indeed it is, but this classification ought not distract us from seeking the properties and methods of the Range object.

The Microsoft Excel Object Model

Range and Font form part of Excel's object hierarchy – the Excel Object Model. Here is a small part of it.

The diagrammatic representation of the Excel Object Model in the VBA Help will vary slightly with Excel version.

We will discuss the Application, Workbook and Worksheet objects in later chapters

The VBA Help is an almost indispensable reference. Don't be discouraged if things are not always easy to find.

The yellow objects are also described as collections by the legend. Collections are groups of objects which have the same properties and methods, which we will also discuss later

Legend

☐ Object and collection
☐ Object only

Click on an object to get Help on that particular object

The Object Model enables us to establish which objects belong to which, but it may be more straightforward to consult the VBA Help's "Applies To" on a particular individual property or method page to establish this

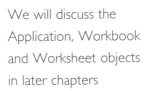

Microsoft Excel Objects

See Also

- Application
  - Workbooks (Workbook)
    - Worksheets (Worksheet) ▶
    - Charts (Chart) ▶
    - DocumentProperties (DocumentProperty)
    - VBProject
    - CustomViews (CustomView)

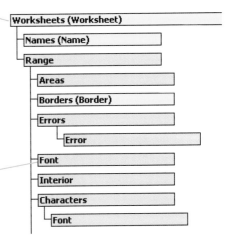

Microsoft Excel Objects (Worksheet)

See Also

- Worksheets (Worksheet)
  - Names (Name)
  - Range
    - Areas
    - Borders (Border)
    - Errors
      - Error
    - Font
    - Interior
    - Characters
      - Font

Bold Property

See Also   Applies To   Example

True if the font is bold. Read/write **Variant**.

Example

Other properties and methods

Formula

The `Formula` property of the `Range` object is used to insert a formula into a cell.

First place a value into cell A1 and then run this code:

```
Private Sub CommandButton1_Click()
Range("B1").Formula = "= A1 * 2"
End Sub
```

Take care not to include a space before the second equal sign

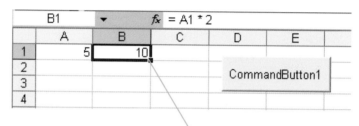

The formula will be placed into cell B1 and the result calculated

Operations using properties are of two types: property read and property write. By assigning some data (a formula in the case above, but usually a value) to the property, we perform a property *write*. On the other hand, as the following piece of code shows, we can also *read* the `Formula` property of the particular `Range` object if the formula is still in place.

```
Private Sub CommandButton1_Click()
Dim x As Variant
x = Range("B1").Formula
MsgBox x
End Sub
```

For a property read, the property is usually on the right hand side of an equal sign (whereas for a write it is usually on the left)

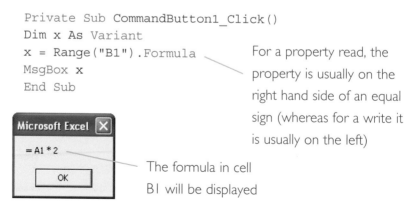

The formula in cell B1 will be displayed

...cont'd

A formula is "copied down" when the single formula is "pasted" into a range of cells as shown below:

```
Private Sub CommandButton1_Click()
Range("B1:B3").Formula = "= A1 * 2"
End Sub
```

The formula automatically "adjusts" down the column

To make all of the formulas in a spreadsheet visible, in the Excel widow press Ctrl+`. Press Ctrl+` again to view the values once more.

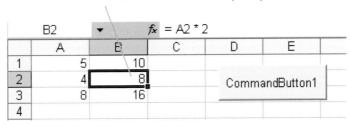

Of course, to prevent the formula from changing when copying down, we could specify an absolute reference.

```
Range("B1:B3").Formula = "=$A$1 * 2"
```

FormulaR1C1

To change the reference style on the spreadsheet (either R1C1 or A1 style), from Excel, choose Tools, Options..., General and check/uncheck R1C1 reference style.

FormulaR1C1 is used in a similar manner to the Formula property, except that FormulaR1C1 must be used in code with R1C1 style. Formula can be used with *both* A1 and R1C1 style. For example, to place a formula in a cell A1 which would refer to the contents of cell C2 (row 2, column 3) we would use:

```
Range("A2").FormulaR1C1 = "= R2C3 * 2 "
```

The use of R1C1 or A1 style in code is independent of which option is currently set for the spreadsheet.

Whereas R2C3 is an absolute reference, R[2]C[3] is relative.

There is really no preference over the use of FormulaR1C1 or Formula. As well as formulas, both can be used to place *values* into a cell. The use of FormulaR1C1 will be seen in code resulting from the use of the macro recorder, in statements such as ActiveCell.FormulaR1C1 = "2" as we will see in Chapter 5.

Address

The Address property will return the address of a particular range. It is a String type.

Selection

The Selection property will return a Range object representing the selected cell or cells. It returns a Range type.

First select some cells on the sheet

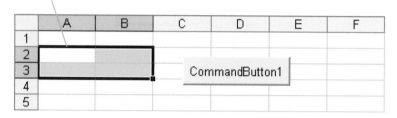

When the code below is run, a message box will appear with the address of the selection.

```
Private Sub CommandButton1_Click()
MsgBox Selection.Address
End Sub
```

The Address of the range selected is returned. At present, it is specified as an absolute reference (the default). See the VBA Help if you require a relative reference

To simply emphasize that the Address property is indeed a String type, for the exercise, we can arbitrarily introduce a variable of String type as shown below to achieve exactly the same result as the code above.

```
Private Sub CommandButton1_Click()
Dim st As String
st = Selection.Address
MsgBox st
End Sub
```

...cont'd

For Excel 97 users: Whenever an attempt is made to change certain properties by means of a command button, ColorIndex being one of them, it is necessary to set the TakeFocusOnClick property of the command button to False. See Chapter 9 on setting command button properties. This issue was resolved for Excel 2000 onwards.

ColorIndex

To change the font color of a spreadsheet cell, we can use the ColorIndex property of the Font object:

```
Private Sub CommandButton1_Click()
Range("A1:A3").Font.ColorIndex= 3
End Sub
```

Running the code above will change the font color of the 3 cells in the range A1:A3 to red

	A	B	C	D
1	5			
2	4			
3	8		CommandButton1	
4				
5				

The value of ColorIndex is the offset of a particular color in the Excel color palette of 56 colors. The respective colors in this palette can be reassigned from the much larger range of colors available overall by using the Colors property (see VBA Help and overleaf for more information), but at any given time, only 56 colors are available. As demonstrated above, at present the color which is at offset 3 is red.

A convenient way of determining the ColorIndex of a particular font is to first apply the font color to a spreadsheet cell, select it and then determine its ColorIndex using a message box to display the value, e.g.

```
MsgBox Selection.Font.ColorIndex
```

You may be surprised to learn that the ColorIndex for the default font of a cell in an Excel spreadsheet is not black, i.e. it is not 1; it has the awkward value of -4105. Fortunately, Excel VBA assigns this value to xlColorIndexAutomatic, an Excel VBA built-in constant, so to change the font color of cell A1 back to "black" we could use:

```
Range("A1").Font.ColorIndex = xlColorIndexAutomatic
```

Color

Font colors can also be assigned using the `Color` property, e.g. to change the font color of cell A1 to green we could use:

```
Range("A1").Font.Color = 65280
```

These values will not seem to follow any pattern unless you are familiar with hexadecimal.

Fortunately, there are two ways of getting assistance with assigning these constant values to the `Color` property.

One way is to use the `RGB` function. The `RGB` function has three numbers corresponding to the red, green and blue components respectively. These three numbers can only take values from 0 to 255, depending on the amount of each of these primary colors, e.g.

```
Range("A1").Font.Color = RGB(0,255,0)
```

would achieve the same result as using the code above, i.e. the cell's font color would be changed to (bright) green.

Secondly, we could use the built-in Excel VBA color constants, e.g.

```
Range("A1").Font.Color = vbGreen
```

The line above will also cause the font color of the cell to be changed to green, exactly as before.

It is interesting to single step the code and hold the mouse cursor over the `vbGreen` constant to reveal its equivalent numerical value.

Don't confuse the Color property which is used to set a color as shown here, with the Colors property which is used to change the default palette, e.g. ActiveWorkbook.Colors(5) = RGB(255, 0, 0) which will change the color with ColorIndex 5 in the palette to red.

```
Private Sub CommandButton1_Click()
Range("A1").Font.Color = vbGreen
End Sub                    vbGreen = 65280
```

Whereas the VBA Help may be a little overpowering when trying to determine the values of these color constants (where they are given as hexadecimal), it may be more convenient to search for them using the Object Browser (press F2 from the VBE).

Object variables

We have seen how to declare and assign variables, e.g.

```
Dim i As Integer
i = 2
```

Similarly, we can declare variables of the generic `Object` type. When assigning an object variable, use the `Set` keyword.

```
Dim r As Object
Set r = Range("B2:C4")
```

It is a common mistake to forget to use Set.

Whereas this code will perform perfectly well, it is more efficient if we are more specific as to the exact type of the object variable, i.e.

```
Dim r As Range
Set r = Range("B2:C4")
```

A `Range` variable is useful when used in combination with the `Cells` property. The cell reference can be specified *relative* to a `Range` as shown here.

```
Private Sub CommandButton1_Click()
Dim r As Range
Set r = Range("B2:C4")
r.Cells(1,2).Select
End Sub
```

The selection will now be made relative to the range r

For illustration, place a border around the range B2:C4

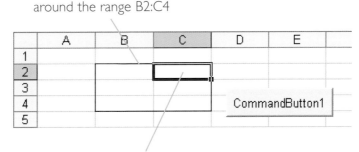

When the code is run, this cell is selected. Cells(1,2) now refers to the cell of the 1st row and 2nd column of the range B2:C4

When `Cells` is used with a single index (and without an object qualifier), it will refer to the cells on a *worksheet*, counting from left to right, e.g.

```
Cells(3).Select
```

would select the third cell of the top row. `Cells` wraps around, so that in the spreadsheet of 256 columns,

```
Cells(257).Select
```

would select the first cell of the second row after wrapping around the first row as shown here.

	A	B	C
1			
2			
3			
4			

It is particularly convenient to use `Cells` with a single index to loop through a defined range. For example the following code will loop through and display the first eight cells of the range A1:A8.

```
Private Sub CommandButton1_Click()
Dim rng As Range
Dim i As Integer
Set rng = Range("A1:A8")
    For i = 1 To 8
    Msgbox rng.Cells(i).Value
    Next i
End Sub
```

The value of the ith cell in the range A1:A8 will be displayed

	A	B	C	D
1	42			
2	35			
3	36			
4	37		CommandButton1	
5	38			
6	39			
7	23			
8	48			
9				

Microsoft Excel

42

OK

To sum numbers according to color

Excel does not have any worksheet functions for dealing with font colors. For example, if we have a list of numbers that we wish to sum or sort according to their color, we will need to write some code. Here we wish to sum red and blue numbers separately, and display the respective totals using a message box.

Place eight numbers in the first column colored red and blue

We want a message box to appear displaying the respective totals

To quickly change the font color of individual cells in Excel, click on a cell containing that color, double click on the Format Painter button on the tool bar, and then click on the cells to which you wish to apply the color.

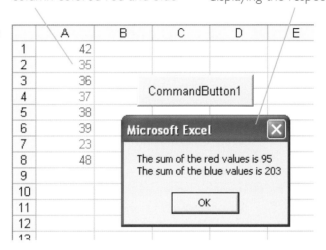

Once again, we will develop our code in easy steps.

1 First modify the code on the previous page (modify the MsgBox line) to display the ColorIndex of the eight consecutive cells by means of the message box as shown below.

If using Excel 97, set TakeFocusOnClick to False when using ColorIndex with a command button.

```
MsgBox rng.Cells(i).Font.ColorIndex
```

Ensure that only the two ColorIndex values 3 and 5 are displayed, otherwise the code overleaf will need to be modified accordingly.

2 The use of Select Case will cater for each of the possible values of ColorIndex. We also need to include the mechanism for summing the cell values, which we can do by using the variables sumRed and sumBlue to keep running totals, which are updated on each pass of the loop.

The complete code to sum numbers according to their color will then be:

```vba
Private Sub CommandButton1_Click()
Dim rng As Range, i As Integer, ci As Integer
Dim num As Single
Dim sumRed As Single, sumBlue As Single
sumRed = 0: sumBlue = 0 'set the totals to zero
Set rng = Range("A1:A8")
   For i = 1 To 8          'do all 8 cells
   ci = rng.Cells(i).Font.ColorIndex
   num = rng.Cells(i).Value
      Select Case ci
      Case 3
      sumRed = sumRed + num
      Case 5
      sumBlue = sumBlue + num
      End Select
   Next i
MsgBox "The sum of the red values is" & _
Str(sumRed) & vbCrLf & _
"The sum of the blue values is" & Str(sumBlue)
End Sub
```

If a red cell is found, the value (num) is added to the red total

Likewise for the blue cell

The line continuation character must include a space before it.

vbCrLf (carriage return-linefeed) is another of the VB built-in constants. It forces the string following to be output onto a new line

As a result of running this program, a message box ought to appear displaying the respective totals.

Microsoft Excel

The sum of the red values is 95
The sum of the blue values is 203

OK

The macro recorder

Not only are you able to write Visual Basic code using the Excel VBE (Visual Basic Editor), but you can get Excel to write it for you using the macro recorder! We learn how to record a macro, and discuss its advantages and shortcomings.

Covers

Chapter Five

To record and run a macro

We will record and run the simplest of macros, a macro which will place a number into a cell when we press a certain key combination.

To record the macro

Our macro will place the number 2 into cell A1 when we press the Ctr+q key combination.

1 Before we start recording, select any cell apart from cell A1. From the Excel menu, choose Tools, Macro, Record New Macro....

2 Accept the default name for the macro. In future you may wish to give it a more meaningful name.

3 Choose This Workbook. Be careful not to select Personal Macro Workbook at this stage.

The key combination used to run the macro is case sensitive.

4 Choose the key combination that we would like to use to run the macro (Ctrl+q).

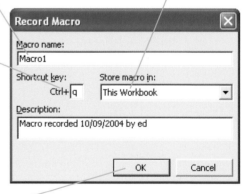

5 Click OK.

The Stop Recording toolbar appears

The macro recorder is recording your every move – mistakes included!

	A	B	C	D	E
1					
2					
3					
4					
5					
6					

6 Click into cell A1, type 2 and then press Enter.

	A	B	C	D	E
1	2				
2					
3					
4					
5					
6					

If you do close the Stop Recording box in error, you will need to choose View, Toolbars, Stop Recording from the Excel menu to switch it back on while the macro is recording!

7 Click the Stop button (the solid blue square).
Do *not* click the Close button (x) to close this box!

Congratulations, you have just recorded a macro.

To run the macro

If the 2 is still in cell A1, delete it.

	A	B	C	D	E
1	2				
2					
3					
4					
5					
6					

If you arrange the Excel and VBE windows on your screen so that you can see both whilst recording a macro, you can see the macro (VBA) code written before your very eyes!

| From Excel, press Ctrl+q. The 2 should appear in cell A1.

That's all it takes to run an Excel macro!

To edit a macro

We will now view and modify the VBA code produced by the macro recorder.

From the Excel menu, choose Tools, Macro, Macros...

The Macro dialog box appears:

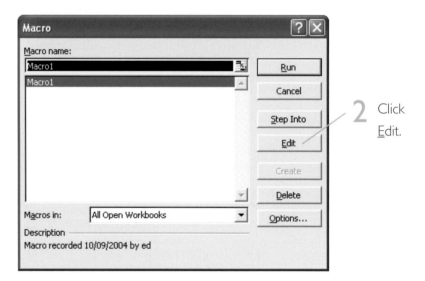

2 Click Edit.

A code module now appears (see next page). Note the name in this case – Module1. Unlike the code modules that we have seen in the past, this is a general purpose code module (generally known as a standard code module) for the whole workbook, whereas the modules that we have seen so far were specific to and only available for that particular worksheet.

Comments have been automatically placed in the code

The Macro Recorder frequently uses Select and ActiveCell (another property which returns a Range object). We will show how this redundancy can be removed below

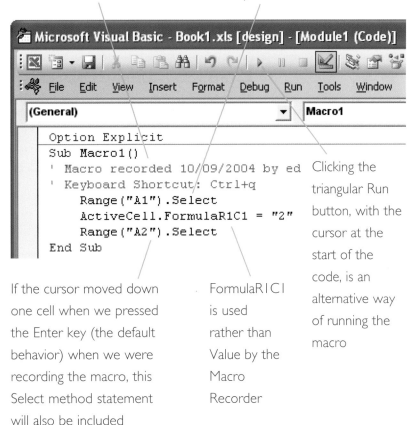

```
Option Explicit
Sub Macro1()
' Macro recorded 10/09/2004 by ed
' Keyboard Shortcut: Ctrl+q
    Range("A1").Select
    ActiveCell.FormulaR1C1 = "2"
    Range("A2").Select
End Sub
```

Clicking the triangular Run button, with the cursor at the start of the code, is an alternative way of running the macro

If the cursor moved down one cell when we pressed the Enter key (the default behavior) when we were recording the macro, this Select method statement will also be included

FormulaR1C1 is used rather than Value by the Macro Recorder

Removing redundancy

Remove `Select` and `ActiveCell` from the macro code and make one line as shown below.

```
Range("A1").FormulaR1C1 = "2"
```

If the macro is run again, the result will be exactly the same, i.e. you will see 2 placed into cell A1 (if it is not already there).

Project Explorer

Project Explorer displays all of the code modules in a project. It can be used to view the code that you have written in the respective code modules, as well as that written by the macro recorder.

1 To view Project Explorer, click View, Project Explorer from the VBE menu or click the Project Explorer button on the VBE toolbar.

You may need to rearrange your windows in the VBE if you wish the Project Explorer window to appear docked as shown.

The VBE windows sometimes refuse to successfully dock as shown. Unfortunately, to resolve this, it is necessary to delete the Dock key value in the Windows Registry (first closing Excel) – not a task for the faint-hearted!

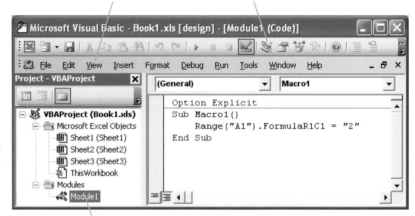

2 Double click on Module1 to see the macro code. This module may or may not appear in a folder, depending on the state of ToggleFolders.

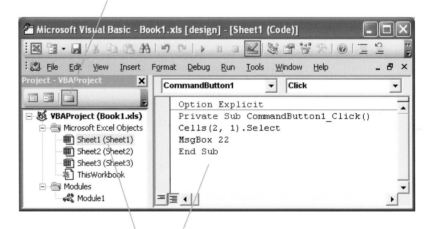

You can also double click on a sheet module to view any worksheet code which may be present

If we were to now record another macro, the code would appear in the same module (in our case Module1). If, on the other hand, we were to start a new session (i.e. close and reopen our Excel workbook), and then record another macro, then a brand new module (Module2 in this case) would appear with the new macro code in it.

The macro recorder is a truly outstanding feature of Excel. It is not present in Access VBA nor stand-alone Visual Basic, which is further reason why Excel is in many ways a preferable environment for learning Visual Basic.

So why don't we just use it all of the time?
Because the macro recorder will not produce code for loops for example, (e.g. For...Next) and other conditional code (e.g. If...Then) which is really what programming is all about!

When should we use the macro recorder?
The macro recorder is invaluable when we need assistance with our code. For example, if we did not know the code needed to change the font color of a cell to red, we could simply change the font color of a cell to red whilst recording a macro, and then inspect the code. All will be revealed if we then turn to the code editor and find a line like this:

The macro recorder can be used to produce a code skeleton in which to place experimental code, in preference to using a command button procedure.

```
Selection.Font.ColorIndex = 3
```

Macros available to other workbooks

We wish to record a macro which will be available not only to the presently open workbook, but to all other workbooks that we might open in future. We will record a simple macro to apply Currency formatting to a cell.

1 Select the cell that you wish to format.

2 From the Excel menu, choose Tools, Macro, Record New Macro....

3 Give the macro a name, e.g. CurrencyFormat.

4 Choose Personal Macro Workbook.

5 Choose the key combination that we would like to use to run our macro (e.g. Ctrl+w).

Record Macro

Macro name:
CurrencyFormat

Shortcut key:
Ctrl+ w

Store macro in:
Personal Macro Workbook

Description:
Macro recorded 10/09/2004 by ed

OK   Cancel

7 Format a cell as Currency (Format, Cells..., Number, Currency, OK) – the cell may or may not have a value in it.

6 Click OK.

8 Click the Stop Recording button.

You may wish to now run the macro and/or view its code.

Project Explorer can be accessed from the VBE by using Ctrl+R.

Project Explorer will show projects associated with more than one workbook.

This all seemed very straightforward, but quite a bit has happened behind the scenes. From the VBE, take a look at Project Explorer.

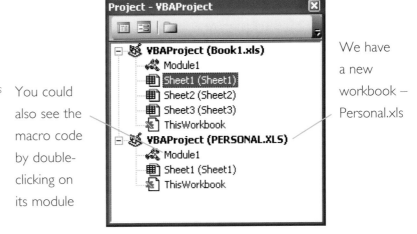

You could also see the macro code by double-clicking on its module

We have a new workbook – Personal.xls

Personal.xls is a hidden workbook which is automatically created when we choose to make macros available to all workbooks. To view Personal.xls, use the Unhide dialog box shown below; choose Window, Unhide... from Excel. If you do unhide it, hide it again.

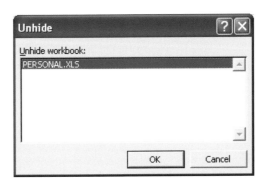

Close the current workbook (save it or not) and close Excel. When asked whether you want to save (the changes to) the Personal Macro Workbook, choose Yes. Personal.xls will now forever be opened automatically as a hidden workbook whenever you start a new workbook (unless you choose to delete it). If we had chosen not to save it, our macros recorded in the Personal Macro Workbook would be lost.

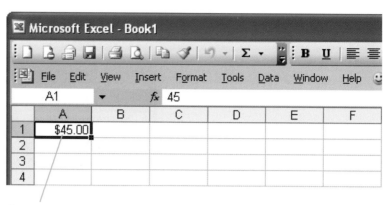

Confirm that the macro will run in any workbook by opening a new workbook and pressing Crtr+w in order to run the macro (to format a cell as Currency)

Having an extra workbook open every time that we start a new workbook may be considered to be a high price to pay for making macros available to all workbooks.

Where is this Personal.xls workbook saved? In the XLStart folder. How can we confirm it is there? Do a file search from Windows: Start, Search etc. – making sure to search for hidden files as well. If we were to delete it from this folder (make sure that Excel is closed first), it will no longer open automatically when we start Excel, but of course all of the macros contained in the Personal.xls will be lost. Since we will need the Personal.xls macros for the next exercise, retain it for the moment.

To run a macro from a toolbar button

We will now place a button on the toolbar and associate it with the macro that we have just written.

1 In order to place a toolbar button on the Excel toolbar, from Excel, choose Tools, Customize...

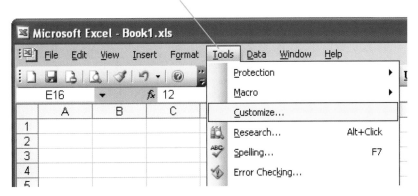

2 Choose the Commands tab.

4 Drag a button from here onto the Excel toolbar.

3 Choose Macros.

5 With the Customize dialog box still open, right-click on the button and chose Assign Macro...

6 Choose our macro and click OK.

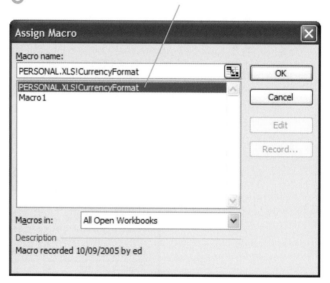

7 Click the Close button on the Customize dialog box.

8 To run the macro, simply choose a cell that we wish to format and click our button on the Excel toolbar. Note that this button will appear on every workbook that you open in future. If you delete Personal.xls, Excel will complain if you click it!
If you wish to remove the button, open the Customize dialog box once again and simply drag it off the toolbar.

The Worksheet object

In this chapter we consider the properties, methods and events of the Worksheet object, and introduce the concept of the collection as it applies to the Worksheet object. We learn that events can be made to trigger by doing something as simple as clicking on a worksheet.

Covers

Chapter Six

Worksheet properties and methods

Each worksheet in an Excel workbook is represented by a corresponding VBA `Worksheet` object. As an object, the `Worksheet` object has properties and methods. This example demonstrates the `Name` property and `Delete` method respectively.

```
Private Sub CommandButton1_Click()
MsgBox ActiveSheet.Name
ActiveSheet.Delete
End Sub
```

When the above code is run, a message box will appear with the name of the current sheet...

... followed by a dialog box asking for confirmation.

When the dialog box appears asking for confirmation, take care to decline lest you irretrievably delete the very worksheet and its module that holds your code!

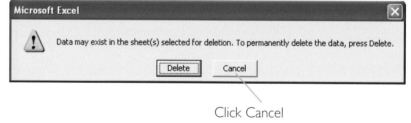

Click Cancel

The `PrintPreview` method can be used to emulate the pressing of the Print Preview button from Excel, e.g.

The PrintOut method can also be used to preview a page (only) by setting the named parameter PreView to True, i.e. ActiveSheet.PrintOut PreView :=True. We will discuss named parameters in Chapter 10.

```
Private Sub CommandButton1_Click()
ActiveSheet.PrintPreview
End Sub
```

Similarly, if we wish to actually print the sheet we could instead use:

```
ActiveSheet.PrintOut
```

Collections

Not all collections are formed by adding "s" to the corresponding object, e.g. Rows is a collection of Range objects whereas Row itself is a property which indicates a row number.

A collection is a group of objects which have the same properties and methods. A collection allows us to deal with the objects as a unit. The name of a collection of a group of objects is almost always, very conveniently specified by adding "s" to the object. For example `Worksheet` objects are contained in the `Worksheets` collection. Each object in a collection can be referenced by an index. A collection is particularly useful for iterating through a group of objects. For example, if we wished to find the respective names of three workbooks, we could use `i` as an index to iterate through the collection as follows:

```
Private Sub CommandButton1_Click()
Dim i As Integer
    For i = 1 To 3
    MsgBox Worksheets(i).Name
    Next i
End Sub
```

3 is the number of worksheets in this workbook

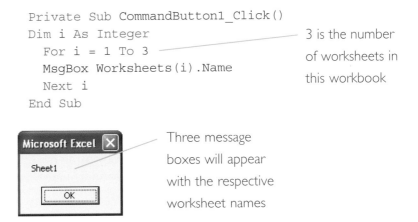

Three message boxes will appear with the respective worksheet names

Note that the index of the `Worksheet` object corresponds to the *order* in which the worksheets appear at the bottom left of the Excel window. This is most important to remember, in case the end user of the spreadsheet decides to swap them around! In anticipation of this, `CodeName` could be used to refer to the sheet in preference to `Name` as we shall see at the end of this chapter.

Try running the above code again, but this time first swap the sheets around so that Sheet2 is the first sheet. Now the first message box to appear should display Sheet2 – the first object in the collection

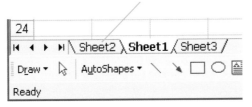

Collection properties and methods

Collections have their own properties and methods.

The Count property reveals the number of items in the collection, e.g.

    Msgbox Worksheets.Count

will indicate the number of worksheets in the Worksheets collection.

Count is particularly useful when we want to loop through a collection as shown below.

```
Private Sub CommandButton1_Click()
Dim i As Integer
For i = 1 To Worksheets.Count
Msgbox Worksheets(i).Name
Next i
End Sub
```

Worksheets.Count specifies the total number of worksheets

Just as we can add a worksheet from Excel (Insert, Worksheet etc.), we can add a new worksheet by using the Add method of the Worksheets collection to add a new Worksheet object to the Worksheets collection, i.e.

    Worksheets.Add

will add a new worksheet before the active worksheet.

The Remove method, in general is used to remove an item from a collection, but it seems that we are only able to remove a Worksheet from the Worksheets collection via the Delete method of the Worksheet object. For example, the following line of code will effectively remove the first worksheet object in our Worksheets collection.

    Worksheets(1).Delete

The first worksheet at the bottom left of the Excel window will be removed

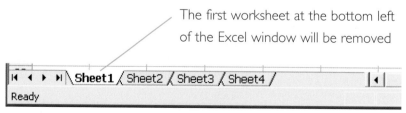

Take care when using a loop to remove items from a collection since as they are deleted, the remainder will continually be renumbered! Hint: If you wish to delete them all, delete them backwards.

If you are not sure what type an object variable should be, use the generic Object type, e.g. Dim wks As Object, but is not recommended if speed of execution is important.

Another quite amazing feature of the collection object is its ability to renumber itself when an object is added or removed.

Accordingly, you will need to keep in mind that `Worksheets(3)` for example, will not remain `Worksheets(3)` if a sheet has been added or removed before it.

We can declare a variable as a `Worksheet` type, just as we can declare variables to be of `Integer` or `Range` type, e.g.

```
Dim wks As Worksheet
```

If a collection is clever enough to know how many items it contains (`Count`), then perhaps we shouldn't have to specify this number at all – and indeed we don't! The `For Each...Next` loop is a special loop which does not require us to specify the number of objects – it will iterate through the collection until it runs out of objects.

```
Private Sub CommandButton1_Click()
Dim wks As Worksheet
   For Each wks In WorkSheets
   MsgBox wks.Index
   Next wks
End Sub
```

The Index numbers of the worksheets will be displayed sequentially

Microsoft Excel ✕

1

OK

`Item` is another of the properties of a collection, but it is a default property and accordingly, `Worksheets(1).Item(1)` for example, can be written equivalently as `Worksheets(1)`, which serves exactly the same purpose.

For example, the following two lines are equivalent:

```
MsgBox WorkSheets.Item(1).Name
```

```
MsgBox WorkSheets(1).Name
```

Cells, columns and rows

Cells

Each individual `Worksheet` can be considered to be composed of cells. Each individual cell is a `Range` object.

To select all of the cells of the first worksheet we could use:

```
Worksheets(1).Cells.Select
```

Cells returns all of the cells of a worksheet

To select the first cell we could use:

```
Worksheets(1).Cells(1).Select
```

Cells(1) is the first cell

Columns

Note that if you wish to Select a range on another worksheet, you must activate the sheet first! e.g.
Worksheets(2).Activate
Worksheets(2).Cells(1).Select

Notice that above we said that the `Worksheet` object "can be" considered to be composed of cells, because it can also be considered to be composed of columns or rows (each of which is a `Range` object) depending on what is convenient at the time!

The `Columns` property returns all of the columns of a particular worksheet. `Columns(2)` for example, would return the second column on a worksheet. We could therefore select column 2 using:

```
Worksheets(1).Columns(2).Select
```

	A	B	C	D	E
1					
2					
3					
4					

Rows

Similarly, the `Rows` property returns all of the rows of a particular worksheet, so we could select the second row of the first worksheet with:

```
Worksheets(1).Rows(2).Select
```

	A	B	C	D	E
1					
2					
3					
4					

Count

Columns is a property which returns a Range object.

It is interesting to use the `Count` property of `Columns` to determine the number of columns on a sheet. Note that we don't bother to specify the worksheet here – it is assumed to be the active worksheet (`ActiveSheet`).

```
MsgBox Columns.Count
```

Similarly, use the `Count` property of `Rows` to determine the number of rows.

```
MsgBox Rows.Count
```

ColumnWidth

`Rows` and `Columns` are themselves properties which return collections of rows and columns respectively. To change the width of all of the columns of a spreadsheet for example, we can take advantage of a collection's ability to deal with all of the objects in the collection as a unit. For example, to change the width of each column of the active sheet we could use

```
Columns.ColumnWidth = 5
```

where 5 is the width of each column in characters. The above is an example of *writing* to a property. Since ColumnWidth is a read/write (variant) we could also *read* the property using:

```
Msgbox Columns.ColumnWidth
```

Worksheet events

As well as having properties and methods, an object can have events. An event is an action that is performed by the user, such as clicking a mouse or pressing a key. An event procedure is code that will trigger (via the operating system) whenever the corresponding event occurs.

To write a worksheet event (Selection_Change)

1 Make sure that Project Explorer is visible and then double click on the sheet name (Sheet1 in this case) to access its code module.

2 Click on the Object drop-down and then select Worksheet.

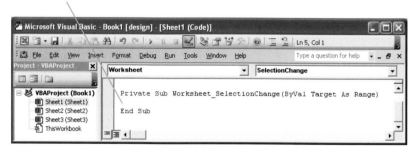

3 The SelectionChange event procedure "template" appears by default . Click in it and write the code shown on the next page. If you inadvertently create another event, delete it and choose the SelectionChange event procedure.

The SelectionChange event is triggered whenever the user changes the selection on the worksheet, for example if the user clicks on another cell on the same worksheet. Like all other Worksheet events, it will only work for that particular worksheet.

Target is the "target" of our mouse click. It is a Range object which is passed (via the operating system) to this event. ByVal concerns the way that objects are passed to procedures and will be explained later

```
Private Sub Worksheet_SelectionChange(ByVal _
Target As Range)
MsgBox Target.Address
End Sub
```

Note the line continuation character shown here which you may not require in your code

4 When the user clicks on another cell, the message box appears displaying the address of the cell that the user clicked on.

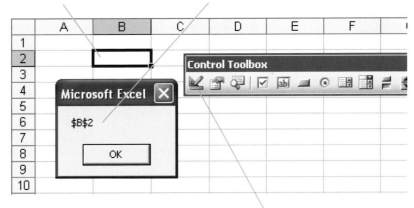

Make sure that the Design Mode button is not depressed – your worksheet event will not fire if it is

Confirm that this event won't trigger for another worksheet, by selecting a cell on another sheet.

The Worksheet_Change event

The Change event occurs when the user physically changes the contents of a cell on the sheet.

Before starting, make sure to comment out or remove the code in the SelectionChange event from the previous example so that it won't trigger when we are testing the new event

If, when you click on the Object box, a default event procedure is placed in your code sheet that you don't want, simply highlight it and delete it.

1 If the code module is not already visible, double-click on the required sheet in Project Explorer as before.

2 Click on the Procedure drop-down and choose the Change event.

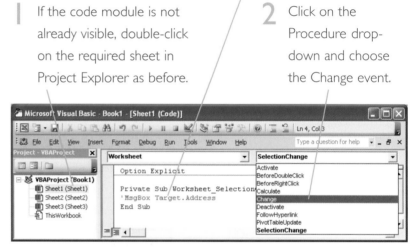

Place some code in the Change event which itself changes the contents of a cell, e.g. Cells(1,1).Value = 2 – you will get a chain reaction. This newly-changed cell will trigger the Change event – will change the cell – will trigger the Change event etc. To halt it press Ctrl+Break. Application.EnableEvents will enable us to prevent this chain reaction as we will see later.

3 Place this code in the Worksheet_Change event procedure.

```
Private Sub Worksheet_Change(ByVal Target As Range)
If Target.Value > 5 Then Target.Font.ColorIndex = 3
End Sub
```

4 Type in some numbers.

	A	B	C
1			
2		4	
3		6	
4			
5			

After a number bigger than 5 is entered, it turns red

If using a version of Excel from 2000 on, make sure that Extend list (data range) formats and formulas is turned off (Tools, Options..., Edit) to avoid spurious formatting effects in this case.

The Worksheet_BeforeRightClick event

BeforeRightClick doesn't mean before you right-click!

`BeforeRightClick` means after the user has right-clicked, but before the right-click event reaches the operating system and is acted upon. The default behavior for the right-click of course, is for the context-sensitive pop-up menu to appear on the spreadsheet. If we do not wish this to occur after a right-click, set the `Cancel` property of the event to `True` as shown below.

```
Private Sub Worksheet_BeforeRightClick _
(ByVal Target As Range, Cancel As Boolean)
Cancel = True
MsgBox "Right Click"
End Sub
```

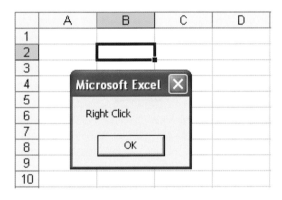

The Worksheet_BeforeDoubleClick event

`BeforeDoubleClick` is very similar to the `BeforeRightClick` event, except of course to raise the event, the user must double-click a cell, and in this case setting `Cancel = True` will cause the default cell editing behavior to be canceled.

BeforeRightClick and BeforeDoubleClick are useful procedures for testing your code as an alternative to the CommandButton1_Click() event.

```
Private Sub Worksheet_BeforeDoubleClick _
(ByVal Target As Range, Cancel As Boolean)
Cancel = True
MsgBox "Double Click"
End Sub
```

The Worksheet_Calculate event

Microsoft Excel Help (not VBE Help) states "By default, Microsoft Excel automatically recalculates formulas when the cells that the formula depends on have changed".

Excel will recalculate automatically only if Calculation is set to Automatic (From Excel, choose Tools, Options..., Calculation, Automatic), otherwise it is necessary to press the F9 key to recalculate (all of) the worksheets.

The Worksheet_Calculate event will trigger whenever a recalculation occurs.

1 Place a value in a cell, and a formula that depends on it in another (see below). Place the Worksheet_Calculate code shown below in the code module of the worksheet.

```
Private Sub Worksheet_Calculate()
MsgBox "Recalculated"
End Sub
```

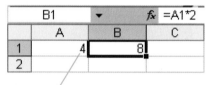

2 Change the value on which the formula depends. The message box should appear, reminding us that a recalculation has just taken place. If your Calculation mode is not set to Automatic, pressing the F9 key will have the same effect.

This Worksheet_Calculate event only triggers when a recalculation occurs on this particular worksheet. What if we want the Calculate event to trigger on any worksheet? We need the Workbook_SheetCalculate event of the Workbook object which we will meet in the next chapter.

Automatic sheet entry

We have below a workbook which contains three sheets. The first sheet is the Invoices sheet which contains records of recent dividend payments for each customer: Caldwell and Crossfire who have their respective account details on the separate, correspondingly-named sheets. We wish to be able to double-click on a customer's name on the Invoice sheet, and have the respective sheets automatically activated, in order that the payments may then be manually entered on that particular sheet.

We wish to double-click on a client name to activate the corresponding sheet

	A	B	C	D
1	Account	Date	Dividend	
2	Caldwell	01/02/2004	243.34	
3	Crossfire	02/02/2004	233.51	
4				
5				

Invoices / Crossfire / Caldwell /

Ready

Place the code below into the `BeforeDoubleClick` event of the Invoices sheet.

```
Private Sub Worksheet_BeforeDoubleClick _
(ByVal Target As Range, Cancel As Boolean)
Cancel = True
Worksheets(Target.Value).Activate
End Sub
```

The value in the target cell will be the name of the client, which corresponds to the name of the sheet to be activated

When we double-click on Caldwell (cell A2) for example, in the Invoices sheet, the Caldwell sheet should become activated as shown:

	A	B	C	D
1	Date	Dividend		
2				
3				
4				
5				

Invoices / Crossfire \ Caldwell /

It would be more useful perhaps, to also automatically update the entries on the chosen sheet. This could best be achieved using the `Offset` property of the `Range` object which will be considered in a later chapter. For the moment, suffice it to say that `Target.Offset(0,1).Value` would return the value contained in the cell which is one cell to the right of a cell that we double-click.

With this knowledge, we can actually *update* the respective sheets as well as choosing them. After double-clicking on the respective names, each of the two sheets ought to be updated with the date and dividend value as is shown here for the Crossfire sheet:

	A	B	C	D
1	Date	Dividend		
2	02/02/2004	233.51		
3				
4				
5				

`|◄ ◄ ► ►|\ Invoices \ Crossfire / Caldwell /`

The following code should achieve that.

```
Private Sub Worksheet_BeforeDoubleClick(ByVal _
Target As Range, Cancel As Boolean)
Cancel = True
Worksheets(Target.Value).Activate
Worksheets(Target.Value).Cells(2, 1).Value = _
Target.Offset(0, 1).Value
Worksheets(Target.Value).Cells(2, 2).Value = _
Target.Offset(0, 2).Value
End Sub
```

Since we are not using the Select method to select a cell on the chosen worksheet, it is not essential that we Activate the sheet, i.e. we could omit the Worksheets(Target.Value).Activate line, unless we want to immediately view/check the new entry.

At present, if we double-click on a cell with no contents, an error will occur. To provide for this, we could either trap the run-time error, or insist by means of a message box that the user double-clicks only the permissible cells. Both of these remedies will be considered later.

Target.Offset(0,2) is the cell which is 2 cells to the right of the cell double-clicked upon on the Invoices sheet, which contains the Dividend value (Offset(0,1) contains the Date)

Target.Value is the name of the worksheet on which the values will be placed. Cells(2,1) and Cells(2,2) is where the Date and Dividend value will be placed respectively on this sheet

Worksheet names

A worksheet has two names, one which can be changed by the user, and one which can only be changed by the programmer. To change the former, of course, we proceed as follows.

From Excel, change the name of the worksheet by double-clicking on the name and typing a new name

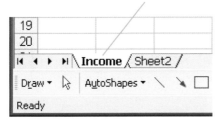

We wish to inspect this new name in the VBE, and to also change the `CodeName`. From the VBE, view the Properties window of the worksheet (choose View, Properties Window).

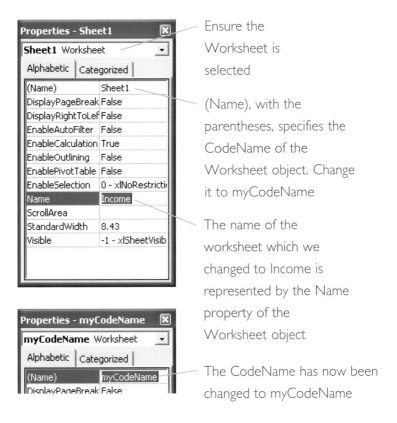

Ensure the Worksheet is selected

(Name), with the parentheses, specifies the CodeName of the Worksheet object. Change it to myCodeName

The name of the worksheet which we changed to Income is represented by the Name property of the Worksheet object

The CodeName has now been changed to myCodeName

Project Explorer can also be used to view the Name and the CodeName. Choose View, Project Explorer.

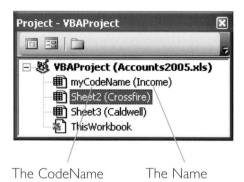

The CodeName   The Name

We are familiar with using the Name property to refer to a worksheet from code – for example to protect a sheet:

```
Private Sub CommandButton1_Click()
Worksheets("Income").Protect
End Sub
```

This of course is equivalent to choosing, Tools, Protection, Protect Sheet... from the Excel window. To unprotect the sheet, choose Tools, Protection, Unprotect Sheet... , or use the Unprotect method from code.

The equivalent using CodeName would be:

```
Private Sub CommandButton1_Click()
myCodeName.Protect
End Sub
```

When writing code, it is good practise to try to use the CodeName to refer to a worksheet rather than the Name. The problem with using the Name is that a user is able to change the name of the sheet, in which case your code will surely fail. Since it is very unlikely that the user will change the CodeName, this is a better bet.

Note that the default name for both the Name and the CodeName are the same initially, e.g. Sheet1, so that for example, Worksheets("Sheet1").Protect and Sheet1.Protect would be equally acceptable!

The Workbook object

By considering the Workbook object as a member of the Workbooks collection, we can employ methods and properties which apply to all open workbooks. By considering the Workbook itself as an object, we can utilize events which can be made to trigger for all the worksheets in a particular workbook.

Covers

Chapter Seven

The Workbooks collection

Just as individual `Worksheet` objects constitute a `Worksheets` collection, individual `Workbook` objects are grouped into a `Workbooks` collection. The `Workbooks` collection represents all of the *currently open* workbooks. The `Workbook` object is the abstract representation of a physical workbook, much the same as a `Worksheet` object is a representation of an actual worksheet. The main purpose of organizing `Workbook` objects into a `Workbooks` collection object, is to enable us to deal with all (open) workbooks as a whole and to be able to easily refer to them individually using an index (just as we saw in the case of the `Worksheets` collection).

1   Create two new workbooks and name (save) them Tax2004.xls and Tax2005.xls respectively. Write the code as shown below in the Command1_Click event of one of the worksheet modules of either workbook, which will iterate through all of the open workbooks (two in this case) and display their respective names.

```
Private Sub CommandButton1_Click()
Dim wkb As Workbook
   For Each wkb In Workbooks
   MsgBox wkb.Name
   Next wkb
End Sub
```

Name is a property of the
Workbook object

2   Run the above code by clicking the command button on the sheet. Message boxes will appear with the names of the workbooks, including the one from which the code was run, in the order that they were opened (or created).

Workbook properties

Path

`Path` describes the location of a workbook (usually on the hard disc).

FullName

`FullName` describes the location and name of a workbook.

The first opened/created workbook has an index of 1

```
Private Sub CommandButton1_Click()
MsgBox Workbooks(1).Name
MsgBox Workbooks("Tax2004.xls").Path
MsgBox Workbooks("Tax2004.xls").FullName
End Sub
```

The code will fail if the named workbook is not open.

The Name of a Workbook can be used as a "key". Don't forget the file extension

When the above code is run, we first get a message box displaying the Workbook Name property...

...followed by a message box displaying the path of the workbook...

The Path of a workbook will be empty if it has not been saved and its (default)
Name will not have an xls extension.

...followed by a message box displaying the path and name (FullName) of the workbook

Workbook/s methods

The `Workbook` object, like all other objects, has methods as well as properties and events.

Close

The `Close` method can be used to close a particular workbook, e.g. the first opened/created workbook as shown here.

```
Private Sub CommandButton1_Click()
Workbooks(1).Close
End Sub
```

`Workbooks.Close` will close all open workbooks. Try it. If there have been changes, of course a prompt will appear.

Open

The `Open` method is used here to open a workbook which is in the active directory (the one that we are currently saving to and opening from). If the file is elsewhere, we would need to specify the file's path and name. This code would be written in one workbook in order to open another.

The code will fail if Tax2005.xls is not in the active directory.

```
Private Sub CommandButton1_Click()
Workbooks.Open("Tax2005.xls")
End Sub
```

Note that `Open` is a method of the `Workbooks` object, not the `Workbook` object.

If you view the IntelliSense drop-down for the Workbook object, other useful methods (and properties) such as Activate, PrintOut, Save and SaveAs etc. appear

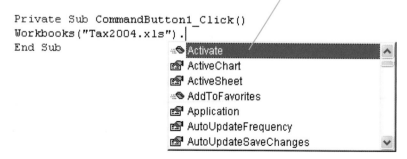

Workbook events

Useful as they are, `Worksheet` events (of the previous chapter), only trigger for the specific worksheet (which contains the module in which the events are written). On the other hand, `Workbook` events will trigger for any worksheet in the workbook.

The Workbook_SheetSelectionChange event

The *Worksheet* event `Worksheet_SelectionChange` was encountered in the previous chapter. It fired whenever we changed a selection on a particular worksheet. On the other hand, the *Workbook* event `Workbook_SheetSelectionChange` will occur whenever we change the selection on *any* worksheet.

We will now write a `Workbook_SheetSelectionChange` event which will produce a message box displaying the name of the worksheet that was clicked upon, along with the address of the cell selected.

Pressing Ctrl+R from the VBE will open Project Explorer.

1 In order to get to the Workbook event procedures, first open Project Explorer.

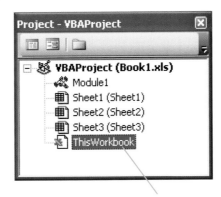

2 Double-click on ThisWorkbook.

The ThisWorkbook code module is "visible" from every worksheet in the workbook, i.e. its code can be run from any sheet in the workbook.

The special ThisWorkbook code module appears as below.

3 Click the Object drop-down and choose Workbook.

4 Click the Procedure drop-down and choose SheetSelectionChange.

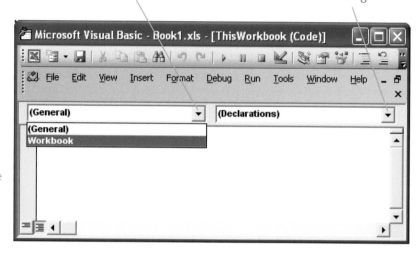

If, when you click on the object drop-down, the default workbook event procedure appears, i.e. Open, simply ignore it or delete it.

5 Write the code in the Workbook_SheetSelectionChange procedure as shown below.

```
Private Sub Workbook_SheetSelectionChange _
(ByVal Sh As Object, ByVal Target As Range)
MsgBox Sh.Name & " " & Target.Address
End Sub
```

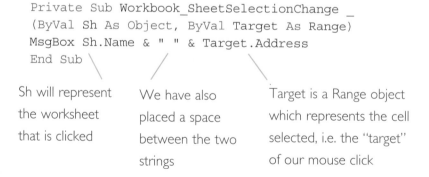

Sh will represent the worksheet that is clicked

We have also placed a space between the two strings

Target is a Range object which represents the cell selected, i.e. the "target" of our mouse click

These variables, Sh and Target are passed to our procedure via the Windows operating system.

6 Return to Excel and click any cell on any sheet. The message box appears as below, displaying both the name of the sheet that was clicked upon, as well as the address of the cell (with a space in between).

Make sure that the Design Mode button on your Control Toolbox is not depressed or else your event won't trigger.

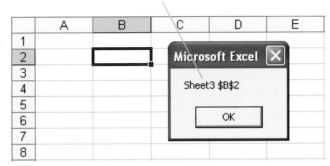

The Workbook_SheetDeactivate event

Comment out or delete any other event code so that it won't trigger as well.

1 Follow the same procedure as before to place code in a Workbook procedure, but this time choose the SheetDeactivate event in the Procedure drop-down and write the code shown.

```
Private Sub Workbook_SheetDeactivate(ByVal _
Sh As Object)
MsgBox Sh.Name
End Sub
```

2 When we choose another sheet in the workbook (e.g. Sheet2), we get a message box displaying the name of the sheet that *was* the active sheet.

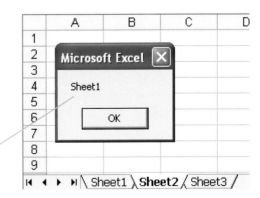

The Workbook_BeforePrint event

This `Workbook` event enables us to specify an operation that will be carried out between choosing the Print (or Print Preview) command and the print operation itself.

Your printer drivers must be installed for Print Preview to work. You also will need to have something on the sheet to print.

For example, we may wish to automatically print a footer at the bottom of each page. This footer, for example, could consist of the file name and its location (the `Workbook`'s `FullName`).

Place the code shown below in the Workbook_BeforePrint procedure.

To determine the necessary code yourself, record a macro to place a footer at the bottom right of the page.

```
Private Sub Workbook_BeforePrint(Cancel As Boolean)
ActiveSheet.PageSetup.RightFooter = _
ThisWorkbook.FullName
End Sub
```

The ThisWorkbook object represents the workbook which contains the code

The ActiveSheet object represents the current worksheet (the sheet about to be printed)

Run the code by clicking the Print Preview button (or the Print button) from Excel.

If you have a carefully designed page footer of your own, it may get overwritten.

The Workbook_BeforePrint triggers, so that you should see the workbook's location and name in the bottom right-hand corner of each page for this particular worksheet.

Click Close to close the Print Preview window.

C:\MyDocs\Tax2004.xls

Note the difference between the Open event and the Open method. The Open method (of the Workbooks object) causes a workbook to open, whereas the Workbook_Open event fires when the workbook opens.

The Workbook_Open event

This event will occur when a workbook opens.

1   Write this code as in the Workbook_Open procedure.

```
Private Sub Workbook_Open()
MsgBox "Don't forget the April deadline"
End Sub
```

2   Close the workbook (save the changes) and open it again. The following message box should appear after the workbook opens.

The Workbook_BeforeClose event

Similarly the Workbook_BeforeClose could be used to respond to the closing of the workbook, e.g. this code will cause a message box to appear after File, Close is chosen from the Excel menu.

```
Private Sub Workbook_BeforeClose(Cancel As Boolean)
MsgBox "Only save the Jan sales figures"
End Sub
```

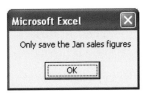

Command bars that we create by code or otherwise, persist, i.e. the next workbook opened will also display them. To avoid this, we could place code in the Workbook_Open procedure to create command bars, and correspondingly place code in the Workbook_BeforeClose to remove them. Not as easy as it sounds!

Workbook in the Excel Object Model

Where in the Excel Object Model hierarchy is the Workbook object located?

The diagrammatic representation of the Excel Object Model in the VBA Help is version specific.

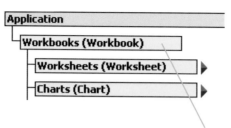

The Workbook object is a member of the Workbooks collection which is located directly beneath the Application object. The Application object, which we will discuss later, represents Excel itself

As previously mentioned, the Excel Object Model is useful when we want to know which objects to place on the left (the parent objects) of our dot operators. Fortunately these parent objects are not always compulsory. For example, recall how we made the font of a cell bold.

```
Range("A1").Font.Bold = True
```

If we were for example, currently working in Sheet1 of the workbook Tax2005.xls, then we could, if we wished to be more specific, specify (redundantly in this case) the worksheet and workbook explicitly as shown below:

```
Workbooks("Tax2005.xls").WorkSheets("Sheet1"). _
Range("A1").Font.Bold = True
```

As we can see from the Excel Object Model, the `Application` object is the parent of the `Workbook` object so that we could also (redundantly) include it as the parent of the Workbook object if so desired, as shown here.

```
Application.Workbooks("Tax2005.xls") _
.WorkSheets("Sheet1").Range("A1").Font.Bold = True
```

In the case we just saw, the specification of the parent object is optional, but specification of the parent objects may sometimes be essential. For example, we may wish to place text on a worksheet different from our active worksheet, or indeed in a workbook different from the current workbook as shown by the code below.

The alternative workbook (Tax2004.xls in this case) would need to be open – recall that the `Workbooks` collection consists only of open workbooks. If it were not open, we could use the `Workbooks.Open` method to open it.

If Tax2004.xls containing a sheet named Sheet2 were not open, an error would occur.

```
Workbooks("Tax2004.xls").WorkSheets("Sheet2"). _
Range("A1").Value = "Income"
```

Parent property

We could use the `TypeName` function to determine the `Parent` of the `Worksheet` as shown here.

```
Private Sub CommandButton1_Click()
MsgBox TypeName(Activesheet.Parent)
End Sub
```

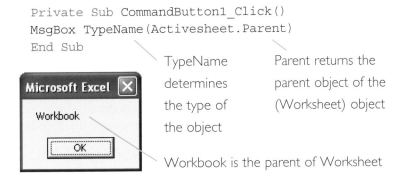

TypeName determines the type of the object

Parent returns the parent object of the (Worksheet) object

Workbook is the parent of Worksheet

Furthermore, we could determine that `Application` is the parent of the parent of the `Worksheet` object, by using:

```
MsgBox TypeName(Activesheet.Parent.Parent)
```

An automatic alert

We have two sales teams, Team1 and Team2. Their respective sales figures are kept on two worksheets named Team1 and Team2 respectively. The total of the sales figures (summed using a SUM formula) appears in the cell B6 on each sheet. If the sum of the sales of either team (i.e. on either sheet) exceeds 20,000, we wish to be alerted as shown below.

We need an event which will trigger when either sheet is recalculated – the Workbook_SheetCalculate event.

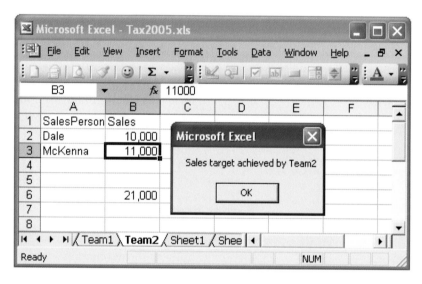

We need to check whether the value of cell B6 on the particular sheet which recalculated exceeded 20,000. This is achieved by testing the value of Sh.Range("B6").Value where Sh will represent the particular worksheet on which the recalculation occurred. When a recalculation does occur (i.e a value upon which a formula depends is changed), this code should cause an alert to appear when the value in cell B6 of either sheet exceeds 20,000.

```
Private Sub Workbook_SheetCalculate(ByVal _
Sh As Object)
If Sh.Range("B6").Value > 20000 Then
MsgBox "Sales target achieved by " & Sh.Name
End If
End Sub
```

Sh represents the sheet (and the name of the team) which caused the recalculation

The Range object

We have already briefly met the Range object. Since the Range object can be used to represent a region on the spreadsheet, it is probably the most important VBA object of all, so in this chapter we will have more to say about how you can use its properties and methods to gain direct control of Excel's functionality.

Covers

Chapter Eight

Columns

We previously saw how the `Columns` property, when applied to the `Worksheet` object, was used to select a whole spreadsheet column. When applied to a `Range` object however, the `Columns` property will return a column of that particular range, e.g.

```
Private Sub CommandButton1_Click()
Range("B2:D4").Columns(2).Select
End Sub
```

will select the second column of the specified range as shown here.

The second column of the range BI:B3 (the range BI:B3 has been formatted here for illustration) is selected

	A	B	C	D	E
1					
2					
3					
4					
5					

The following code will format the cells (make them blue and bold) of the first column of a table.

ColorIndex for blue

```
Private Sub CommandButton1_Click()
Range("B2:D4").Columns(1).Font.ColorIndex = 5
Range("B2:D4").Columns(1).Font.Bold = True
End Sub
```

	A	B	C	D	E
1					
2		January	24,380	34,550	
3		February	25,345	34,450	
4		March	35,700	28,340	
5					

Rows

Similarly, the Rows property can be used to return the row of a specified range, e.g.

```
Private Sub CommandButton1_Click()
Range("B2:D4").Rows(2).Select
End Sub
```

The second row of the range B1:B3 is selected

	A	B	C	D	E
1					
2					
3					
4					
5					

We could, for example, place formulas into the bottom row of a table as shown below to add the values directly above and embolden the result.

```
Private Sub CommandButton1_Click()
  With Range("B2:D4").Rows(3)
  .Formula = "=Sum(B2:B3)"
  .Font.Bold = True
  End With
End Sub
```

Note the use of With ... End With which simply saves the retyping of Range("B2:D4").Rows(3). With ... End With is of course more useful with larger programs.

B4	▼	_fx_ =SUM(B2:B3)		
	A	B	C	D	E
1					
2		54,500	24,380	34,550	
3		65,000	25,345	34,450	
4		119,500	49,725	69,000	
5					

The formula to sum each column has been copied across to each cell in row 3 of the table

Practical examples

Example 1

We wish to find the maximum value in a list of numbers.

First place some numbers in the range
B1:B6 whose maximum we wish to find

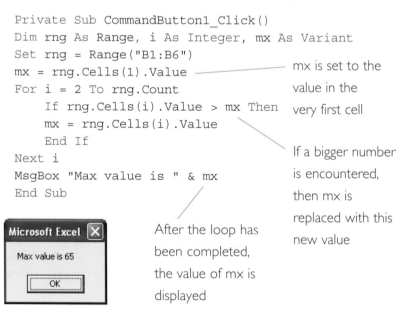

One way of finding the maximum is as follows. First set a temporary maximum variable (mx) to the value of the first cell, and then iterate through the remainder. If a number larger than mx is encountered, ascribe that value to mx, thus replacing mx with the "maximum so far". Move down the list, repeating the process.

```
Private Sub CommandButton1_Click()
Dim rng As Range, i As Integer, mx As Variant
Set rng = Range("B1:B6")
mx = rng.Cells(1).Value
For i = 2 To rng.Count
    If rng.Cells(i).Value > mx Then
    mx = rng.Cells(i).Value
    End If
Next i
MsgBox "Max value is " & mx
End Sub
```

mx is set to the value in the very first cell

If a bigger number is encountered, then mx is replaced with this new value

After the loop has been completed, the value of mx is displayed

This use of a `Range` variable (`rng` in this case), allows us to easily specify another range if desired, i.e. we can easily change the line

```
Set rng = Range("B1:B6")
```

to specify a new range, e.g.

```
Set rng = Range("A1:A6")
```

which contains a set of numbers whose maximum we now wish to find. Conveniently, `rng.Count` in the program code would automatically adjust to represent the number of cells in this new range.

Minimizing the number of fixed constants in program code improves program maintainability and "forward compatibility".

Similarly, if we wished to select a range manually before running the code we could use:

```
Set rng = Selection
```

Example 2

In this second example, using the same column of numbers as in the previous example, we wish to change the font color of cells to blue if they have a value of 50 or more.

The ColorIndex for blue will be 5 only for the default palette, i.e. if the palette has not been changed using the Colors property.

```
Private Sub CommandButton1_Click()
Dim rng As Range, cl As Range
Set rng = Range("B1:B6")
For Each cl In rng
  If cl.Value >= 50 Then
  cl.Font.ColorIndex = 5
  End If
Next cl
End Sub
```

An individual cell (cl) is also a Range object

If the value in the cell is greater than or equal to 50, then make it blue

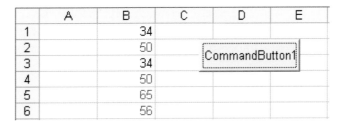

	A	B	C	D	E
1		34			
2		50		CommandButton1	
3		34			
4		50			
5		65			
6		56			

Value

We have previously used the `Value` property for single values. A little surprisingly, the `Value` property can also conveniently be used to accommodate multiple values. Copying a set of values to a new location using the `Range` object with the `Value` property is simplicity itself.

	A	B	C	D	E
1					
2	1	2			
3	3	4			
4					
5	CommandButton1				
6					
7					

To transfer the values shown above to the range D4:E5, we would use:

```
Private Sub CommandButton1_Click()
Range("D4:E5").Value = Range("A2:B3").Value
End Sub
```

	A	B	C	D	E
1					
2	1	2			
3	3	4			
4				1	2
5	CommandButton1			3	4
6					

Whereas `Value` is a default property of the `Range` object, it cannot be omitted in this case – at least not on the right hand side (lest we attempt to put one `Range` object equal to the other).

We can also (redundantly) include the `Cells` property which simply returns all of the cells (themselves `Range` objects) of the `Range` object, as shown below to produce exactly the same result.

```
Range("D4:E5").Cells.Value = _
Range("A2:B3").Cells.Value
```

Copy and Paste methods

It is of interest to record a macro to perform the same copy operation, but using the Excel Copy and Paste commands.

The result of recording a macro to copy the values can be seen below. Note the VBA Copy and Paste methods which result. We could incorporate these methods in our own code (along with Cut if necessary) to transfer values, but the technique utilizing Range.Value which we saw previously is much more efficient and straightforward.

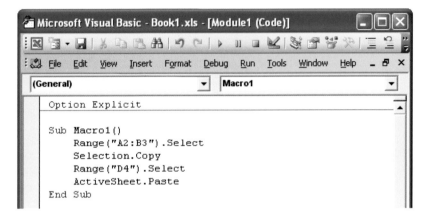

```
Microsoft Visual Basic - Book1.xls - [Module1 (Code)]

File   Edit   View   Insert   Format   Debug   Run   Tools   Window   Help

(General)                              Macro1

Option Explicit

Sub Macro1()
    Range("A2:B3").Select
    Selection.Copy
    Range("D4").Select
    ActiveSheet.Paste
End Sub
```

	A	B	C	D	E
1					
2	1	2			
3	3	4			
4				1	2
5				3	4
6					

CurrentRegion

According to the VBA Help, "The current region is a range bounded by any combination of blank rows and blank columns", i.e. the rectangular region around a group of cells.

When using Excel, we can select the current region by placing our cell cursor anywhere in the region, e.g. cell A1, and pressing the Ctrl+Shift+* key combination

	A	B	C	D	E
1	12				
2		21			
3			44		
4					
5					

The same effect as above could be achieved from VBA using:

```
Range("B1").CurrentRegion.Select
```

CurrentRegion is useful when we don't know in advance, the exact boundaries of the range that our code will be asked to deal with.

For example, say that we want to write a program that will change the font color of a range of cells which contain numbers (as distinct from text), blue as shown below.

	A	B	C	D	E
1		Sales			
2		23.34			
3		Deposits	CommandButton1		
4		34.32			
5		45.56			
6		Divs			
7		12.45			
8					

The following code, which utilizes CurrentRegion, should do just that. The IsNumeric function tests whether a cell's contents is numeric, e.g. IsNumeric(23.34) would return True since 23.34 is numeric, whereas IsNumeric("Divs") would return False.

```
Private Sub CommandButton1_Click()
Dim rng As Range, cl As Range
Set rng = Range("B1").CurrentRegion
For Each cl In rng.Cells
    If IsNumeric(cl.Value) Then
    cl.Font.ColorIndex = 5
    End If
Next cl
End Sub
```

Any cell in the range B1:B7 could be chosen as the "seed" for CurrentRegion

The cell will be colored blue if it is numeric

Note that instead of `rng.Cells`, we might equally just have `rng`. The advantage of using `CurrentRegion` is that the user could make additions to the data, contiguous with the current data and no alteration to the code would be necessary before running it. All numeric values will be turned blue as shown below.

	A	B	C	D	E
1		Sales			
2		23.34			
3		Deposits			
4		34.32	CommandButton1		
5		45.56			
6		Divs			
7		12.45			
8		Interest			
9		14.54			
10					

Data can be added before clicking the button whereupon these numbers should turn blue as well

If, rather than color the numeric values blue, we wished to color the non-numeric values blue, we could use:

```
If Not IsNumeric(cl.Value) Then ...
```

If we wished to manually select a cell in our column of numbers before running the code, rather than specifying a "seed" cell in code, we could replace the corresponding line above with:

```
Set rng = Selection.CurrentRegion
```

UsedRange

UsedRange is a property which returns the range of used cells on a sheet. More specifically, it returns a range bounded by the rectangle whose corners are the most extreme cells. In the example below, these corners are the top-left and bottom-right cells.

```
Private Sub CommandButton1_Click()
ActiveSheet.UsedRange.Select
End Sub
```

The top-left cell forms the top-left corner of the UsedRange rectangle

	A	B	C	D	E
1					
2		23	66		
3			55		
4			77	34	
5					
6					
7		CommandButton1			
8					

The bottom-right cell forms the bottom-right corner of the UsedRange rectangle

UsedRange is a property of the Worksheet object and not of the Range object, but it returns a Range object. UsedRange has shortcomings and should be used with care. For example, if a cell is formatted as bold, and then made unbold, as distinct from clearing the formatting using Edit, Clear, Formats (and any content removed), it is unfortunately still considered as a used cell, and UsedRange would include it in its rectangular boundary.

UsedRange is not always reliable.

The End property of the Range object can be used to ascertain the boundaries of a range, e.g.

```
Range("C2").End(xlDown).Select
```

would select cell C4 in the example data above, i.e. the cell at the bottom of the region containing C2 (the equivalent of manually selecting cell C2 and pressing the End key along with the down arrow key). See Help on the End property for more details.

Offset

The Offset property will return a Range which has the same size, but which is offset by a number of rows and columns, e.g. Offset(4,1) will return a new Range object with the same dimensions, but offset four rows down and one column across.

```
Private Sub CommandButton1_Click()
Range("B2:D4").Offset(4,1).Select
End Sub
```

The range offset by 4 rows and 1 column from the original range is selected

This new range at present has no "permanence". Accordingly, we could set a variable equal to the new Range object as follows:

```
Dim rng As Range
Set rng = Range("B2:D4").Offset(4,1)
```

Specifying only one index will cause the range to be offset by that number of rows, e.g.

```
Set rng = Range("B2:D4").Offset(4)
```

will return a Range moved down four rows.

To offset by a number of columns only, we can either use zero as the first parameter, or omit it altogether, e.g. these two lines of code are equivalent and either will return a range offset by one column.

```
Set rng = Range("B2:D4").Offset(0,1)
```

```
Set rng = Range("B2:D4").Offset(,1)
```

Using Offset, we could for example, emulate/extend the behavior of the Excel VLOOKUP worksheet function. With reference to the table of numbers below, we could display the Amount corresponding to "dfg" using the code shown.

	A	B	C	D	E	F
1						
2		**Amount**	**Code**			
3		23.32	asd			
4		31.32	des	CommandButton1		
5		34.43	dfg			
6		21.32	erg			
7						

```
Private Sub CommandButton1_Click()
Dim rng As Range, code As Variant
Dim i As Integer
code = "dfg"
Set rng = Range("C3:C6")
  For i = 1 To rng.Count
    If rng.Cells(i).Value = code Then
    MsgBox rng.Cells(i).Offset(0,-1).Value
    End If
  Next i
End Sub
```

The value which is one cell to the left of the cell containing "dfg" is displayed

When the code above is run, a message box displaying the amount corresponding to "dfg" should appear.

When the code above is run, a message box displaying the amount corresponding to "dfg" should appear.

Resize

The Resize property will physically change the size of a range to a specified number of rows and columns. The top left cell of the new range remains fixed in place; it is the "anchor point" about which the range is contracted or expanded.

```
Private Sub CommandButton1_Click()
Range("B2:D4").Resize(2,2).Select
End Sub
```

The original range (here formatted with a border), is contracted to 2 rows and 2 columns in total size. The top left cell remains as the "anchor point"

Specifying only one index will cause the range to be resized to that specified number of rows, e.g. Resize(1) will return a range of one row only. We could set a variable to such a new Range object (and select it) as shown:

```
Private Sub CommandButton1_Click()
Dim rng As Range
Set rng = Range("B2:D4").Resize(1)
rng.Select
End Sub
```

To resize to one column for example, we could simply omit any row specification and use Resize(, 1).

A dynamic selection

We wish to be able to click among *any* rectangular group of cells and then click a command button on the sheet...

	A	B	C	D	E
1					
2					
3		45.63	23.43	23.21	
4		34.67	34.23	45.32	
5		23.43	34.45	45.32	
6					

...whereupon the row beneath the cells will be selected.

	A	B	C	D	E
1					
2					
3		45.63	23.43	23.21	
4		34.67	34.23	45.32	
5		23.43	34.45	45.32	
6					
7					

Once again we will write and test our code in easy steps.

Place a command button on the sheet and write some code in its procedure which will simply select the CurrentRegion around the cell that the user clicks upon.

```
Private Sub CommandButton1_Click()
Dim rng As Range
Set rng = Selection.CurrentRegion
rng.Select
End Sub
```

	A	B	C	D
1				
2				
3		45.63	23.43	23.21
4		34.67	34.23	45.32
5		23.43	34.45	45.32
6				

After selecting a cell containing data and running the code, the current region is selected

2 Include code in the command button procedure to increase the number of rows in the range by one (and select it).

```
Private Sub CommandButton1_Click()
Dim rng As Range
Set rng = Selection.CurrentRegion
Set rng = rng.Resize(rng.Rows.Count + 1)
rng.Select
End Sub
```

Select a cell in the table before clicking the command button to run the program.

rng is redefined

rngRows.Count will be 3 when execution reaches this line (and 4 immediately after)

	A	B	C	D	E
1					
2					
3		45.63	23.43	23.31	
4		34.67	34.23	45.32	
5		23.43	34.45	45.32	
6					
7					

3 Change the line of code to select the last row of this new range.

```
Private Sub CommandButton1_Click()
Dim rng As Range
Set rng = Selection.CurrentRegion
Set rng = rng.Resize(rng.Rows.Count + 1)
rng.Rows(rng.Rows.Count).Select
End Sub
```

rngRows.Count will be 4 after resizing

	A	B	C	D
1				
2				
3		45.63	23.43	23.21
4		34.67	34.23	45.32
5		23.43	34.45	45.32
6				
7				

When a cell in the table is selected and the command button clicked, the last row will be selected

This code should work for any sized table, anywhere on the sheet.

Intersect

The intersection of two ranges is the region where they meet.

Borders have been placed around the ranges whose intersection we wish to find

This code will color the intersection of the two ranges.

```
Private Sub CommandButton1_Click()
Intersect(Range("B2:D4"),Range("D3:F5")) _
.Interior.ColorIndex = 33
End Sub
```

Interior is used when we wish to apply a solid color to the cells' interior. ColorIndex 33 is Sky Blue in the default palette

When the program is run, the range intersection is colored blue

Union

The union of two ranges is the "amalgamation" of the two ranges.

Modify the previous code to that shown below (replace Intersect with Union).

```
Private Sub CommandButton1_Click()
Union(Range("B2:D4"),Range("D3:F5")) _
.Interior.ColorIndex = 33
End Sub
```

When the command button is clicked, the union is colored blue

Intersect and Union are methods which return Range objects, so we could assign Range variables as shown.

```
Dim rng1 As Range, rng2 As Range
Set rng1 = Intersect(Range("B2:D4"),Range("D3:F5"))
Set rng2 = Union(Range("B2:D4"),Range("D3:F5"))
```

To test a selection

The objective here is to ensure that a user will click in a certain range. If the user does not, a message box will appear, requesting that the correct range be selected.

```
Private Sub Worksheet_SelectionChange(ByVal _
Target As Range)
Dim rng As Range
Set rng = Range("B2:D4")
   If Intersect(rng, Target) Is Nothing Then
   MsgBox "Please select a cell in the range " & _
   rng.Address
   Else
   MsgBox "OK"
   End If
End Sub
```

If there is no intersection, the range will be Nothing

If the user clicks on a cell which is not in the required range, a reminder appears

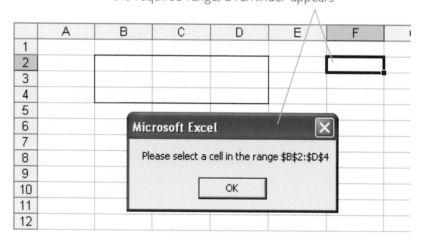

To ensure that the user selects only a *single* cell, we could include this code just before the Else statement.

```
ElseIf Target.Cells.Count <> 1 Then
MsgBox "Please select a single cell"
```

ElseIf provides *another* alternative to the Else, i.e. if the user does either thing wrong, the If or the ElseIf will be chosen, whereas if the user makes a correct selection, Else will be chosen.

The Areas collection

According to the VBA Help, "Areas is a collection of the areas, or contiguous blocks of cells, within a selection. There is no single Area object; individual members of the `Areas` collection are `Range` objects".

On an Excel spreadsheet, when we make one selection and then hold down the Ctrl key to make another, we are creating two areas

	A	B	C	D	E	F
1						
2						
3						
4						
5						

Note carefully the placement of the quotation marks.

The equivalent of this in code would be:

```
Range("B2:B3,D2:E3").Select
```

The two members of this `Areas` collection have index values of 1 and 2 respectively, i.e. `Areas(1)` and `Areas(2)`. Correspondingly, the `Count` property of the `Areas` collection returns the number of these discrete `Range` objects in the collection – in this case 2.

For example, the following code will cause the respective addresses of the two areas to be displayed.

```
Private Sub CommandButton1_Click()
Dim rng As Range, i As Integer
Set rng = Range("B2:B3,D2:E3")
  For i = 1 To rng.Areas.Count
  MsgBox rng.Areas(i).Address
  Next i
End Sub
```

rng.Areas.Count is 2

When the code is run, the address of each area is displayed

As a practical example, we wish to ensure that a user makes a selection of exactly two single cells (using the Ctrl key).

	A	B	C	D	E
1		**SalePerson**		**Sales**	
2					
3		Dale		2387	
4		McKenna		4540	
5					

The Selection object represents the user's choice of one or more areas

If a selection of more or less than two cells is made

```
Private Sub CommandButton1_Click()
If Selection.Areas.Count <> 2 Then
MsgBox "You must make exactly 2 selections"
ElseIf Selection.Areas(1).Cells.Count <> 1 Or _
Selection.Areas(2).Cells.Count <> 1 Then
MsgBox "You must select single cells"
Else
MsgBox "OK"
End If
End Sub
```

If either range has more than 1 cell

For example, if more than one cell is selected in one of the areas and the command button then clicked...

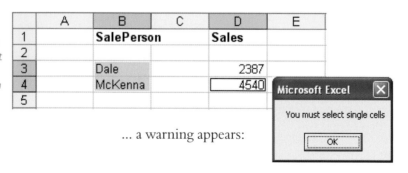

... a warning appears:

To further ensure that the selections were from the correct column and the same row, we could check the Column and Row properties respectively, e.g. Selection.Areas(1).Column and Selection.Areas(1).Row.

ActiveX controls

This chapter describes controls such as text boxes, combo boxes and option buttons which can be placed on the worksheet to improve functionality.

Covers

Chapter Nine

Command button

Controls found on the Control Toolbox (shown below) are ActiveX controls. We have already met one ActiveX control – the CommandButton object.

If you hold your mouse cursor steady over the buttons on the Control Toolbox, the types of ActiveX controls will be revealed (You may wish to draw a few of these on your sheet)

Check Box

We have met the Click event of the CommandButton control. These controls are objects, and accordingly, besides events, have properties and methods. For example, we can change the Caption property of a CommandButton object using this code:

```
Private Sub CommandButton1_Click()
CommandButton1.Caption = "Enabled"
End Sub
```

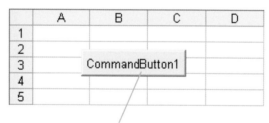

When we click on the command button...

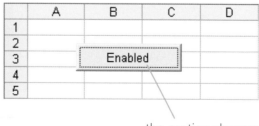

...the caption changes

Changing a property at design-time

So far we have seen how to change a property while the program was running – at run-time. It is also possible to change properties before we run the program – at design-time – as shown below. It is particularly desirable to change the captions of command buttons if we have more than one, in order to distinguish their function, e.g.

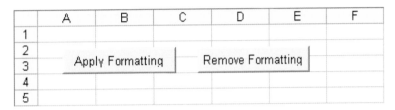

Place two command buttons on a sheet and access the Properties Window from the VBE by clicking on the Properties Window button (or choosing View, Properties Window from the VBE menu).

A quick way of getting the Properties window of the CommandButton from the Excel window is to right-click on the command button (in design mode) and choose Properties.

Make sure that you are in design mode in order to be able to view the CommandButtons in the Properties Window drop-down.

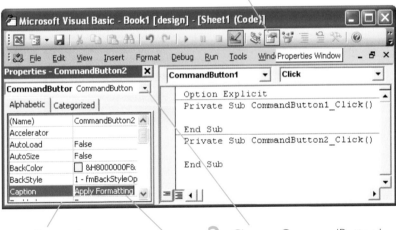

Your Properties Window may or may not be docked as shown

2 Choose CommandButton1 from the drop-down.

3 Change the Caption property to Apply Formatting as shown.

4 Repeat (from Step 2) for the second CommandButton's Caption property. Change it to Remove Formatting.

The Caption property is simply the text which appears on the button. The Name property on the other hand, is how the CommandButton object is programmatically identified. In the previous example shown here again, the Name property of the CommandButton object was CommandButton1.

```
Private Sub CommandButton1_Click()
CommandButton1.Caption = "Enabled"
End Sub
```

CommandButton1 is the Name of the ComandButton control

We will now change the Name property of our two command buttons at design-time. The Properties Window should still be visible.

From the Properties Window, change the Name properties of the corresponding command buttons to cmdApplyFormat and cmdRemoveFormat respectively.

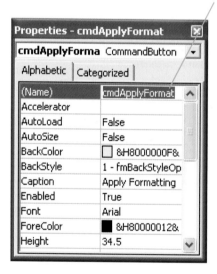

2 From the Excel window, double-click on the first command button (ensuring that you are still in design mode). Repeat for the second command button. The respective code procedures will appear in the VBE as shown.

It is also possible to create the respective Click procedures by simply selecting them in the object drop-down

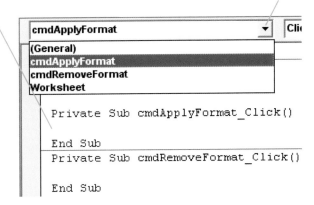

If CommandButton1 or CommandButton2 procedures have been inadvertently created, either ignore or delete them.

Giving the respective CommandButton objects appropriate Names of course enables us to more easily identify the respective procedures. This becomes more useful as programs become larger. We can now place appropriate code in the two procedures as shown.

```
Private Sub cmdApplyFormat_Click()
Selection.Font.ColorIndex = 3
End Sub
```

Insert code into the first procedure which will set the font color of selected cells red.

```
Private Sub cmdRemoveFormat_Click()
Selection.ClearFormats
End Sub
```

2 Insert code into the second procedure which will clear the formatting of the selected cells.

Exit design mode. To demonstrate the program's versatility, we
will apply formatting to a multiple selection rather than just a
single selection. First place some numbers on the sheet which we
wish to selectively format as shown below.

3 Make a multiple selection (using the Ctrl key) and
then click the Apply Formatting button.

	A	B	C	D	E
1					
2					
3	Apply Formatting			Remove Formatting	
4					
5	34				
6	34				
7	54				
8	45				
9					

In this example, the 1st, 3rd and 4th
cells will be formatted (made red)

4 To clear the formatting, make the same
selection and then click the Remove
Formatting button.

	A	B	C	D	E
1					
2					
3	Apply Formatting			Remove Formatting	
4					
5	34				
6	34				
7	54				
8	45				
9					

All of the cells' font color should now return to the default.

Text box

We will now place a text box control onto a sheet, and use it to display some text when a command button is clicked. First place a command button on the sheet and then...

Text Box

1   Click the text box control button on the Control Toolbox.

2   Draw a text box on the sheet.

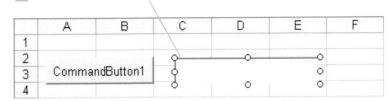

3   Right-click on the text box on the sheet and choose Properties. In the Properties box, change the Name property to txtSales. As an expedience, you may wish to now copy (Ctr+C) this Name and later paste it into your code (see over) to reduce the prospect of a typo.

4 Write this code in the CommandButton procedure.

```
Private Sub CommandButton1_Click()
txtSales.Text = "Sales Results are good"
End Sub
```

In order to see the properties of a particular control, make sure that the control is selected.

txtSales is now the Name by which the text box can be referred to in the program – at least in this particular code module. Text is a property of the text box control. You can see it listed in the Properties box for this text box. It is the default property of the TextBox object and could therefore be omitted.

Omitting default properties is not recommended. For one thing your code is less readable, but could also lead to ambiguity.

5 After exiting design mode, click the command button. The text should appear in the text box.

	A	B	C	D	E
1					
2					
3	CommandButton1		Sales Results are good		
4					

We have thus seen how to give a control (the TextBox control) a name by which we can later refer to it. It would have been perfectly OK to leave the name as the default (TextBox1 in our case), and use that name to subsequently refer to our TextBox control.

If, instead of transferring data *to* our text box, we wished to transfer input data *from* our text box into a spreadsheet cell, we could for example use:

```
Cells(1,1).Value = txtSales.Text
```

To test this code we need to exit design mode and make sure that there is some text in the text box first.

Text boxes are more useful when they are placed on a user form, which we will discuss later.

Spin button

We will place a spin button control on the sheet which will be used to increment and decrement an invoice number in a spreadsheet cell (B2) by utilizing the SpinUp and SpinDown events of the spin button.

1 Use the Control Toolbox to draw a spin button control on the sheet.

	A	B	C
1			
2	Invoice no.		
3			
4			
5			
6			
7			

2 Double-click on the spin button control. The (default) SpinButton1_Change() event procedure will be created. This is the event which responds to the "up" or the "down" arrows being clicked. We want to be more specific. Delete (or ignore) this event procedure.

3 Make sure that SpinButton1 is chosen in the Object drop-down. Choose the SpinUp and SpinDown events from the Procedure drop-down (you may need to delete the SpinButton1_Change() event again) and write the code in the respective procedures as shown.

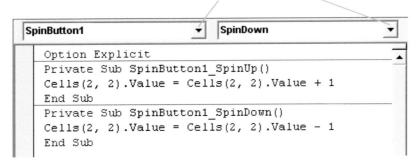

```
SpinButton1            ▼    SpinDown              ▼

    Option Explicit
    Private Sub SpinButton1_SpinUp()
    Cells(2, 2).Value = Cells(2, 2).Value + 1
    End Sub
    Private Sub SpinButton1_SpinDown()
    Cells(2, 2).Value = Cells(2, 2).Value - 1
    End Sub
```

4 From Excel, make sure that the Design Mode button is not depressed and click on the "up" and "down" arrows of the spin button. The value in cell B2 should be incremented and decremented.

	A	B	C
1			
2	Invoice no.	52	
3			
4			
5			
6			

Before trying this, make sure that you delete/ comment the SpinButton1_SpinUp and SpinButton1_SpinDown event code.

For these experimental purposes, the initialization code could simply be placed in a command button procedure. More practically, initialization code could be placed in the Worksheet_Activate or Workbook_Open procedure etc. If the Workbook event is chosen, make sure that SpinButton is qualified by the Worksheet, e.g. Worksheets(1).SpinButton1 etc.

We could achieve the same effect by utilizing the spin button's built-in `Value` property, which is automatically incremented and decremented upon clicking the spin button's "up" and "down" arrows respectively. Using this method we can utilize the `Min` and `Max` properties – the minimum and maximum values that `Value` can take – which can be set at design-time – or at run-time using code such as:

```
SpinButton1.Max = 200
SpinButton1.Min = 100
```

and similarly, the incremental value can be altered from the default of 1 by changing the `SmallChange` property (at design-time or run-time e.g. `SpinButton1.SmallChange = 5`).

The `Value` could then be displayed in the cell using:

```
Private Sub SpinButton1_Change()
Cells(2,2).Value = SpinButton1.Value
End Sub
```

In this case, the value displayed in the cell could only change from 100 to 200, in increments determined by the value of `SmallChange`.

Check box

Place two check boxes on a sheet. Double-click on one, and from the VBE choose the Change event procedure from the Procedure drop-down. You may wish to delete the default Click event procedures as they appear. Choose the other check box object from Object drop-down, choose its Change event and write the respective code in each as shown below.

```
Private Sub CheckBox1_Change()
Range("D3").Value = CheckBox1.Value
End Sub
Private Sub CheckBox2_Change()
Range("D6").Value = CheckBox2.Value
End Sub
```

2 From Excel, exit design mode and click the respective check boxes. The corresponding Value properties will appear in column D – True corresponding to checked, and False corresponding to unchecked. Note that the check boxes (compared to option buttons which we will meet soon) act independently, i.e. checking/unchecking one has no effect on the state of the other.

	A	B	C	D	E
1					
2					
3		☑ CheckBox1		TRUE	
4					
5					
6		☑ CheckBox2		TRUE	
7					

Option buttons

These are almost identical to check boxes, but there is one major difference. When we change one, the other changes automatically.

1 Place two option buttons on a sheet – without any code. Exit design mode and choose one by clicking it. Click on the other button and the former button changes state automatically.

Since we have not yet assigned a button to appear selected by default (i.e. its Value has not been set to True), you will need to manually select one of the option buttons first when the program first runs.

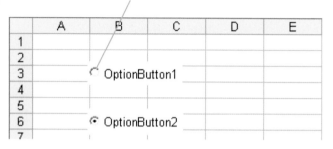

	A	B	C	D	E
1					
2					
3		○ OptionButton1			
4					
5					
6		◉ OptionButton2			
7					

You may wish to delete the default event (Click) procedures if they appear.

2 Revert to design mode and double-click on one option button. Choose the Change event for each one and write the respective code as shown.

```
Private Sub OptionButton1_Change()
Range("D3").Value = OptionButton1.Value
End Sub
Private Sub OptionButton2_Change()
Range("D6").Value = OptionButton2.Value
End Sub
```

3 Exit design mode and select one of the options. *Both* values in column D change, since (unlike a check box) changing one option button will cause the other to change – thereby causing the Change event to trigger in the other as well.

	A	B	C	D	E
1					
2					
3		◉ OptionButton1		TRUE	
4					
5					
6		○ OptionButton2		FALSE	
7					

Combo box

Our simple combo will provide a choice of three items in its drop-down. The combo will be populated with items provided from a list in Column D on the sheet. When an item is chosen from the combo drop-down, it will be made to appear in B5.

1 Using the Control Toolbox, draw a combo box on a sheet and place three items in column D as shown.

	A	B	C	D	E
1				Stock	
2				Expenses	
3				Dividends	
4					
5					

2 Right-click on the combo box (still in design mode) and choose Properties.

The result of our combo choice is to appear in B5

3 In the Properties box, set the ListFillRange to D1:D3 which is the range that will be used to provide the combo box's alternative choices. Set the LinkedCell property to B5 which is the cell we have chosen to display the choice made.

LinkedCell	B5
ListFillRange	D1:D3

4 From the Excel spreadsheet exit design mode, click on the combo drop-down and make a choice.

	A	B	C	D	E
1				Stock	
2				Expenses	
3				Dividends	
4		Stock			
5		Expenses			
6		Dividends			

Make sure that your combo box is not covering cell B5!

5 The choice that we made from the combo drop-down should appear in cell B5 as required.

	A	B	C	D	E
1				Stock	
2		Expenses ▼		Expenses	
3				Dividends	
4					
5		Expenses			
6					

More advanced combo box features

To change to design mode click the Design Mode button on the Control Toolbox.

6 We wish to make a choice from two columns. Place the extra data in column E. In design mode, change ListFillRange to D1:E3 and the ColumnCount property to 2. Increase the box width to cater for the extra column by dragging it. Exit design mode.

	A	B	C	D	E
1				Stock	2600
2	Dividends			▼ Expenses	2400
3	Stock	2600		Dividends	1600
4	Expenses	2400			
5	Dividends	1600			
6					

Two columns appear since ColumnCount is 2.

7 We now want the value from the second column rather than the first to appear in B5, so change the BoundColumn property of the combo box to 2. The BoundColumn is the column in the ListFillRange from which the corresponding choice will be made, e.g. if Dividends is selected, 1600 will appear in B5.

To have only the first column appear in the drop-down, set the ColumnWidths property to 1cm;0cm.

	A	B	C	D	E
1				Stock	2600
2	Dividends			▼ Expenses	2400
3				Dividends	1600
4					
5		1600			
6					

Using option buttons

We will use two option buttons to enable us to choose the name of the worksheet which is to be copied into another workbook. Make two workbooks, Company.xls with two sheets named 2004 and 2005, and Analysis.xls with a sheet named Import.

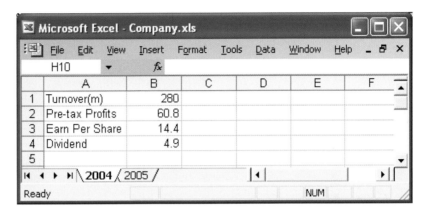

By choosing an option and clicking the button, the required sheet ought to be copied from Company.xls into the current workbook.

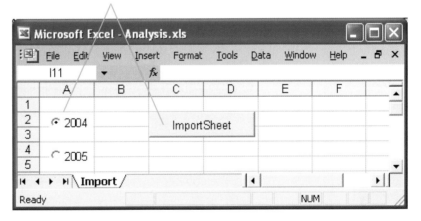

1   Place a command button on the Import sheet. Change its Caption to ImportSheet and its Name to cmdImportSheet.

2   Place two option buttons on this same sheet. Change their Captions to 2004 and 2005 respectively. Leave the Names as the default, OptionButton1 and OptionButton2.

3 Double-click on the command button and write this code.

```
Private Sub cmdImportSheet_Click()
Dim shName As String
    If OptionButton1.Value = True Then
    shName = OptionButton1.Caption
    ElseIf OptionButton2.Value = True Then
    shName = OptionButton2.Caption
    End If
Workbooks("Company.xls").Worksheets(shName).Copy _
After:= ThisWorkbook.Worksheets(Worksheets.Count)
End Sub
```

The sheet, shName is to be copied in

Use variables like Worksheet.Count (rather than 1 in this case) if we wish to ensure that the sheet is placed last – in case there happens to be more than one worksheet in the current workbook.

A colon and equal sign identifies After as a named parameter (discussed later)

Company.xls is the workbook from which the sheet will be copied

Copy is a method of the Worksheet object

4 Make sure that both workbooks are open. After selecting a year and clicking the ImportSheet button...

If you don't select an option on first running the program, an error will occur. To avoid this, one option button could be made the default choice by setting its Value property to True at design-time.

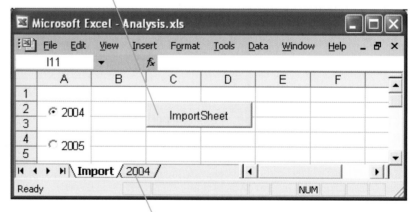

...you should find that the selected sheet has been copied from Company.xls to this workbook.

Procedures

Procedures allow us to compartmentalize and organize our code. We discuss the two main types, subs and functions along with their practical use.

Covers

Chapter Ten

Subs

Procedures are self-contained blocks of code. Procedures become more useful as program size increases. They are of two main types – subs and functions. As we will see, the difference between a sub and a function is that a function can return a value whereas a sub cannot.

Writing a sub

Write this code.

```
Option Explicit
Private Sub CommandButton1_Click()
Square
End Sub

Sub Square()
Dim x As Double
x = 3
x = x ^ 2
MsgBox x
End Sub
```

Square is the name of our sub

As we type "sub Square" and then press Enter, as well as being capitalized, parentheses and End Sub (formatted blue) appear automatically

The `Square` statement in the `CommandButton` procedure has the effect of "calling" the sub. The called procedure simply squares 3 to give 9, which is then displayed by the message box.

Generally speaking, in the course of program development, it is useful to be able to "wrap" code which has been tried and tested into subs (or functions) with identifiable names, and place them outside the main calling program. That way, our main code area should consist of a series of procedure calls (with recognizable names) with the corresponding encapsulated procedures placed after the main program area.

Passing a value to a sub

At present our sub can only square 3. We could modify it so that it could square any number by passing the number to be squared to the sub as follows.

```
Option Explicit
Private Sub CommandButton1_Click()
Square 3
End Sub

Sub Square(x As Double)
x = x ^ 2
MsgBox x
End Sub
```

3 is passed to x

Use Debug to single step (F8) to watch the transfer of program control.

x As Double is the equivalent of Dim x as Double

The variable which accepts the passed value (x in this case), is known as a parameter. Strictly speaking, the 3 which is passed is known as an argument, but both are often referred to as parameters

Change the line

```
Square 3
```

to

```
Square 4
```

to show that another value can be passed. The result, of course, in the latter case, should be that 16 is displayed.

Functions

Functions differ from subs in that they can *return* a value.

Writing a function

Modify the code as shown. Note that after `Function` is typed, `End Function` appears automatically!

```
Option Explicit
Private Sub CommandButton1_Click()
Dim y As Double
y = Square(3)
MsgBox y ——————— This time, the value is
End Sub            returned to y and displayed

Function Square(x As Double) As Double
x = x ^ 2
Square = x
End Function
```

The name of the function (Square) is always "repeated" (usually at the end of the function) and usually put equal to what is to be returned (in this case x)

The return type (also Double) is also specified when using a function. If it is omitted, a Variant return type is assumed

Microsoft Excel

9

OK

A function name invariably appears on the "right-hand-side" of an expression, e.g. y = Square(3) or MsgBox Square(3).

Note that we could replace the command button code with:

```
Private Sub CommandButton1_Click()
MsgBox Square(3)
End Sub
```

We can even include our function name in an expression such as

```
MsgBox 2 * Square(3)
```

in which case we could regard the function name as a variable with value 9, so that 18 would be displayed. Try it.

Passing ByRef and ByVal

Modify the code as shown to pass a variable rather than a constant.

```
Option Explicit
Private Sub CommandButton1_Click()
Dim v As Double
v = 3
MsgBox 2 * Square(v)
End Sub

Function Square(x As Double) As Double
x = x ^ 2
Square = x
End Function
```

The variable v is being passed to the function

Although discussed in relation to functions, ByVal and ByRef have exactly the same effect when used with subs.

After `MsgBox 2 * Square(v)`, which causes 18 to be displayed, include the line `MsgBox v` in order to display the value of v.

Passing a variable to a function or a sub ByRef (by reference), can permanently change the variable passed, whereas passing ByVal (by value) cannot.

When the program is run and 18 has been displayed as expected, quite surprisingly, the value of v is displayed as 9, not 3, i.e. the value of v has been permanently changed (squared) by the function to 9. Reverse remote control!

Include `ByRef` in the corresponding line above so that it becomes:

```
Function Square(ByRef x As Double) As Double
```

It won't make any difference, `ByRef` is the default.

ByRef is the default. Your variables may unintentionally get changed permanently if they are passed by ByRef.

Now change the `ByRef` to `ByVal` so that it becomes:

```
Function Square(ByVal x As Double) As Double
```

`ByVal` ensures that the value is passed by value and not modified inside the procedure.

Technically speaking, ByRef causes the actual memory address of a variable to be passed to the procedure, whereas ByVal causes a copy of the variable to be passed.

This time, when the code is run (and after the 18 has been displayed), the value of v is displayed as 3 and shown to be unchanged after the function call

Using a sub

As an example, we wish to color any 2's which appear in a set of numbers red. We will pass the 2, along with the range to be searched to a sub which we will call ColorCells.

We will search the range A1:A6 and color any 2's found red

	A	B	C	D	E
1	3				
2	2				
3	5	CommandButton1			
4	2				
5	4				
6	2				
7					

Commas are used to separate arguments

Two arguments are passed. The range to be searched is passed to rng

```
Private Sub CommandButton1_Click()
ColorCells 2, Range("A1:A6")
End Sub

Sub ColorCells(x As Variant, rng As Range)
Dim cl As Range
   For Each cl In rng
     If cl.Value = x Then cl.Font.ColorIndex = 3
   Next cl
End Sub
```

Note that the 2 has been passed as a Variant. This would allow us to search for text as well as a number if we wished.

The advantage of using a procedure here is that we can easily change the number that we are searching for, as well as the range that we are searching. Whereas we have searched a column of numbers, it is possible to search any range, and also carry out more than one search, so that we would use the same procedure and modify our calling code to something like this:

```
Private Sub CommandButton1_Click()
ColorCells 2, Range("A1:A6")
ColorCells 4, Range("C1:D4")
End Sub
```

Using a function

As an example, we wish to find the number of 2's in a certain range. We will pass the 2, along with the range to be searched, to a function which we will call `FindNum`. As shown below, we use a function rather than a sub, since we wish to *return* the number of 2's found to the calling procedure.

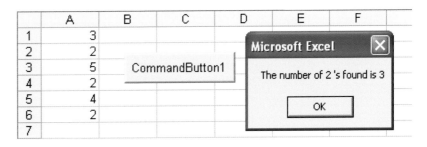

 The spurious space on the left-hand-side introduced by Str (in this case on the left-hand-side of the 3), can be avoided by using CStr instead of Str.

```
Private Sub CommandButton1_Click()
Dim num As Integer, fnd As Variant
fnd = 2
num = FindNum(fnd, Range("A1:A6"))
MsgBox "The number of " & fnd & _
  " 's found is" & Str(num)
End Sub

Function FindNum(x As Variant, rng As Range) _
As Integer
Dim c As Integer, cl As Range
c = 0
    For Each cl In rng
    If cl.Value = x Then c = c + 1
    Next cl
FindNum = c
End Function
```

num is the number of occurrences of fnd

Increment the counter if a 2 found

FindNum is the number of occurrences of x which is passed back to num

Summary

 Use subs and functions wherever possible to organize your code – just like the professionals.

When using functions:
- Use the same function name to return the value, e.g. `FindNum = ...`
- Use parentheses when passing the arguments, e.g. `FindNum(fnd, Range("A1:A6"))` [not with a sub].
- Specify the return type, e.g. `As Integer` as above.

Variable scope

The scope of a variable determines where in the program it is valid. A variable is only "known" at the "level" at which it is declared. This code below will fail with the message shown. Try it.

```
Option Explicit
Private Sub CommandButton1_Click()
sub1
sub2
End Sub

Sub sub1()
Dim i As Integer
i = 1
End Sub

Sub sub2()
i = 2
End Sub
```

Microsoft Visual Basic

⚠ Compile error:

Variable not defined

OK   Help

Code is "compiled" (converted) before being run

The problem is that i is not known in the second procedure, since it was declared in the first procedure only

Include a `Dim` statement in the second procedure as well, as shown below. It is important to realize that the second `i` variable is thereby completely independent of the `i` in the first procedure.

```
Option Explicit
Private Sub CommandButton1_Click()
sub1
sub2
End Sub

Sub sub1()
Dim i As Integer
i = 1
Msgbox i
End Sub

Sub sub2()
Dim i As Integer
i = 2
Msgbox i
End Sub
```

Microsoft Excel

1

OK

Microsoft Excel

2

OK

Each i in this case has procedure-level scope.

What if we did want the `i` in the first procedure to also be known, and retain its value, in the second procedure? We need to declare it in the General Declarations section (at the top of the module).

Remove the `Dim` statements from each sub and modify the code as shown below.

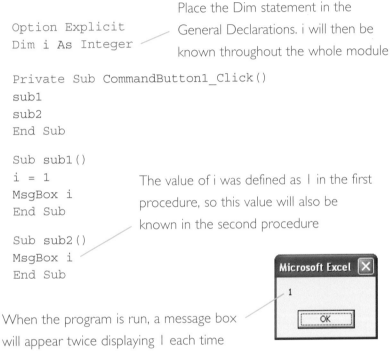

```
Option Explicit
Dim i As Integer
```
Place the Dim statement in the General Declarations. i will then be known throughout the whole module

```
Private Sub CommandButton1_Click()
sub1
sub2
End Sub

Sub sub1()
i = 1
MsgBox i
End Sub
```
The value of i was defined as 1 in the first procedure, so this value will also be known in the second procedure

```
Sub sub2()
MsgBox i
End Sub
```

When the program is run, a message box will appear twice displaying 1 each time

It is very strongly recommended that variables are declared as locally as possible, resisting the strong temptation to use the easy option of module-level variables as above, where the variable is declared outside the procedures that use it (in the General Declarations). One alternative to using module-level or global variables is to pass variables as arguments from one sub to another.

A global variable is one which is declared in a standard code module using Public instead of Dim, e.g. Public i as Integer. Such a variable would then be available to every module (and accordingly every procedure) in the program. Try it. You will need to define the variable (e.g. i = 3) in a procedure.

The objective of a programmer is not only to write a program that works, but to make contingency for when it doesn't. Declaring variables as locally as possible is one of these contingencies. Using `Option Explicit` is another. Knowing precisely where variables are declared and defined helps us to localize the source of any potential errors that may occur.

To color the minimum value

This program will color the smallest value in a selected set of numbers blue. Since the range variable is declared at module level (in the General Declarations), it will be available to all command button procedures in that module, and the selection need not be repeated before clicking the second button to clear the formatting.

Change the Names and Captions of command buttons using the Properties window.

```
Option Explicit
Dim rng As Range
Private Sub cmdFindMin_Click()
Dim i As Integer, mn As Single
Dim c As Integer
Set rng = Selection
mn = rng.Cells(1).Value
c = 1
For i = 2 To rng.Count
    If rng.Cells(i).Value < mn Then
    mn = rng.Cells(i).Value
    c = i
    End If
Next i
rng.Cells(c).Font.ColorIndex = 5
End Sub


Private Sub cmdClearFormats_Click()
rng.Cells.ClearFormats
End Sub
```

After declaration in the General Declarations, the Range variable is defined in the first procedure

After the index (c) of the cell containing the smallest value has been determined, it is used to color that particular cell blue

rng will also be known in this procedure

Don't click the Clear Formats button without first clicking Find Min button.

First select the range, and then click the Find Min button. The minimum value (22 in this case) should be colored blue

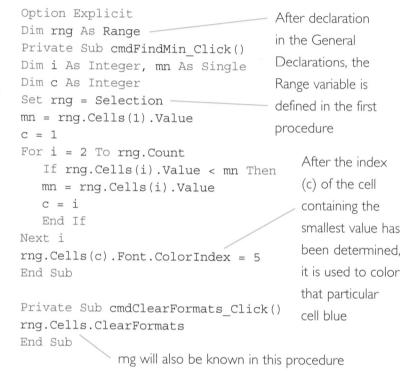

Since rng has module-level scope, there is no need to re-select the range before clicking Clear Formats

Variable lifetime

Lifetime determines where in the program the value of a variable is remembered. If we declare a variable in a procedure using `Static` instead of `Dim`, the variable value will be remembered next time the procedure is called. First we'll *not* use `Static`.

```
Private Sub CommandButton1_Click()
Dim i As Integer
MsgBox i
i = i + 1
End Sub
```

Each time that the command button is clicked, the same value of i (0) appears. The effect of Dim is to set the value back to 0 each time that the button is clicked

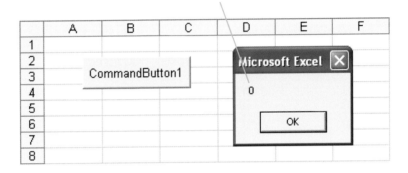

Now change `Dim` to `Static`.

```
Private Sub CommandButton1_Click()
Static i As Integer
i = i + 1
MsgBox i
End Sub
```

Static ensures that the value is remembered from the last time that the procedure was called

If we now continue to click the command button, the value displayed will be incremented by one each time

If the workbook is closed (saved), and reopened, the value of i is forgotten, i.e. it resets to 0.

The MsgBox function

We have met the MsgBox statement, e.g. MsgBox "Click". We could regard this as calling the built-in MsgBox sub and passing it the parameter "Click". MsgBox can also be used as a function, whereby a value is returned, e.g.

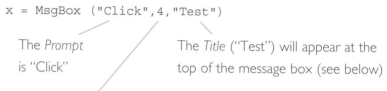

```
x = MsgBox ("Click",4,"Test")
```

The *Prompt* is "Click"

The *Title* ("Test") will appear at the top of the message box (see below)

The *Buttons* value of 4 determines that two buttons, Yes and No will appear on the message box (see the VBE Help for more details)

Type in the code as shown below:

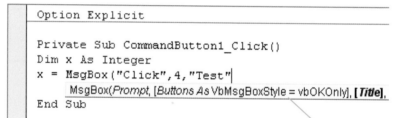

```
Option Explicit

Private Sub CommandButton1_Click()
Dim x As Integer
x = MsgBox("Click",4,"Test"|
    MsgBox(Prompt, [Buttons As VbMsgBoxStyle = vbOKOnly], [Title],
End Sub
```

As we type into the VBE, Auto Quick Info provides a guide to the correct syntax (as well as listing the vb constants available)

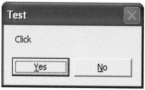

Title is Test
Prompt is Click
Buttons is Yes/No

The value of x returned is determined by the button pressed. If Yes is clicked, the value returned is 6 (vbYes). If No is clicked, the value returned is 7 (vbNo). To confirm this, you may wish to use another MsgBox statement to display the value of x.

```
x = MsgBox ("Click",4,"Test")
MsgBox x
```

Named parameters

Rather than omit the Buttons argument to accept the default, we could use a Buttons value of 0 (vbOKOnly).

What if we did not want to specify Yes/No buttons but instead accept the default of an OK button? We could omit the `Buttons` argument altogether as follows.

```
x = MsgBox("Click", , "Test")
```

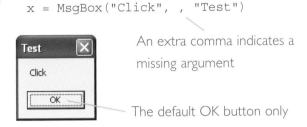

An extra comma indicates a missing argument

The default OK button only

Keeping the arguments in strict order, and providing the required extra commas, can be a little tedious – especially as the number of parameters becomes larger. Named parameters obviates this. The equivalent of the above, using named parameters is:

Always include the colon with the equal sign when using named parameters.

```
x = MsgBox(Prompt:="Click", Title:="Test")
```

Note that if named parameters are used, the order of the arguments no longer matters, e.g. the following statement would be equivalent to the above:

```
x = MsgBox(Title:="Test", Prompt:="Click")
```

In a practical situation, we could test for the returned value. For example, if we wish to confirm that we want to delete the contents of the cells in a selection, we could use:

```
Private Sub CommandButton1_Click()
Dim x As Integer
x = MsgBox(Prompt:="Delete the cell contents?", _
Buttons:=vbYesNo)
    If x = vbYes Then
    Selection.ClearContents
    End If
    'otherwise do nothing
End Sub
```

User defined functions

If we write a function in a standard code module, it can be called from Excel just as we would call a normal worksheet function.

1 From the VBE menu, select Insert, Module.

2 Write this function code in the module to perform a simple currency conversion.

```
Function doll(st As Single) As Single
Dim rate As Single
rate = 1.5
doll = st * rate
End Function
```

It is possible to write code to automatically download the relevant up-to-date exchange rate from the Internet.

3 Type an = sign, followed by the name of our function, along with the source cell reference.

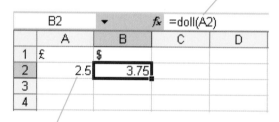

4 If a sterling amount is now entered into A2, the equivalent dollar amount will immediately appear in B2.

Writing the user defined function (UDF) in a standard code module (as well as being essential) immediately qualifies the function as being available for any sheet in the workbook.

Limitations

Only user defined functions can be written – not user defined subs.

User defined functions are very useful for providing your user with encapsulated code which the user can access by simply typing the function name into the formula bar as we have seen, but they have restrictions. Foremost of these is that UDFs cannot be used to change the *structure* of the spreadsheet in any way. This means that not only can we not change the *formatting* of any cells, a UDF cannot be used to place a *value* in a cell. Worse still, we may not get any indication of the error if we try!

UDFs can be used (subject to their limitations) rather than CommandButton procedures to test your code.

Using arrays

Arrays are useful for holding data. In this chapter we consider the different types of array and how they can be manipulated. We also introduce other objects which can relate to, and take advantage of their succinctness as well as employ a technique to warn if their capacity is exceeded.

Covers

Chapter Eleven

1-D arrays

An array is a set of indexed variables. The variables could be Integers, Variants, etc. but must be of a single type. One-dimensional arrays have only one index which is used to assign and access the individual elements. For example, we could define an array of three Strings as shown below.

This Dim declaration reserves space in memory for 3 String elements, indexed from 1 to 3

```
Option Explicit
Dim Company(1 to 3) As String
Private Sub CommandButton1_Click()
Company(1) = "Business Systems"
Company(2) = "Best Image"
Company(3) = "Analytical Systems"
End Sub
```

Variables declared in the General Declarations have module-level scope.

Note that the declaration Dim Company(1 to 3) As String in this case has been placed in the General Declarations area rather than inside the command button procedure, in anticipation of making the array available to other (command button) procedures in that module. To display the third element of the array for example, (using a second command button) we could use:

An error will occur in our example if the first command button is not clicked (to initialize the array) before clicking the second.

```
Private Sub CommandButton2_Click()
MsgBox Company(3)
End Sub
```

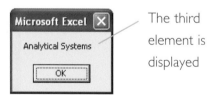

The third element is displayed

A major advantage of storing variables in an array is that they can be conveniently processed using a loop. For example, if we wished to attach the same string to each element in the array, using a 3rd command button, we could use:

```
Private Sub CommandButton3_Click()
Dim i As Integer
   For i = 1 To 3
   Company(i) = Company(i) & " Ltd"
   Next i
End Sub
```
Strings are concatenated

Similarly, we could conveniently display all of these array elements using a simple loop (modifying the code in button 2) as shown below.

```
Private Sub CommandButton2_Click()
Dim i As Integer
   For i = 1 To 3
   MsgBox Company(i)
   Next i
End Sub
```

After clicking the three command buttons (in the order 1, 3 and then 2), the amended names will be displayed

Microsoft Excel ⊠	Microsoft Excel ⊠	Microsoft Excel ⊠
Business Systems Ltd	Best Image Ltd	Analytical Systems Ltd
OK	OK	OK

Instead of declaring our array using:

```
Dim Company(1 to 3) As String
```

we could use:

```
Dim Company(3) As String
```

This will give us an element for free! – element zero – in this case Company(0). We could assign another company name to Company(0), but on the other hand, we may wish to ignore element zero altogether, in order to be consistent with the indexing of Excel spreadsheet cells (which of course do not have zero rows or columns). To officially signal the absence of element zero, we may wish to specify Option Base 1 in the General Declarations, in which case all arrays (at least in that code module) will now be 1-based rather than 0-based.

VB arrays are zero-based by default. Use Option Base 1 in the General Declarations if you wish your arrays to be one-based.

2-D arrays

2-D arrays have one index which denotes the row, and one index which denotes the column, and therefore can be likened to the Excel spreadsheet structure itself. For example, to input the range of spreadsheet entries shown below to an array,

	A	B	
1	Business Systems	29 Highgrove rd	
2	Best Image	31 Curtin Ave	
3	Analytical Systems	28 Drayton Gdns	
4			

If an array is declared inside a procedure, it will only be available to that procedure, wheras if it is declared in the General Declarations, it will be available to all procedures in that module.

we would use: rows   columns

```
Dim Company(1 To 3, 1 To 2) As String
Dim rw As Integer, cl As Integer
    For rw = 1 To 3
        For cl = 1 To 2
        Company(rw, cl) = Cells(rw, cl).Value
        Next cl
    Next rw
```

To access elements of a 2-D array, use two indices, e.g. Company(1,2) would access the element in row one and column two.

The alternative declaration of `Dim Company(3, 2) As String`, would reserve space for an array of 4 rows and 3 columns, i.e. the elements `Company(0,0)`, `Company(0,1)`, `Company(1,0)` etc. would also be available (unless we specify `Option Base 1`).

VB arrays can have more than 2 (up to 60) dimensions. For example, we could declare a 3-D array which could be used to represent cells in a single workbook of 3 sheets using
`Dim BookValues(3, 1000, 256) As Variant`
for a workbook containing 3 sheets of 1000 rows and 256 columns of data – elements with 0 index simply being ignored.

UBound

Minimize the number of fixed constants in your code by using functions such as UBound.

As an alternative to `For rw = 1 To 3` we could use `For rw = 1 To UBound(Company,1)`, where `UBound(Company,1)` indicates the size of the 1st dimension of the `Company` array which is 3 in this case – the number of rows. Similarly `UBound(Company,2)` would represent the value of the 2nd dimension which is 2 in this case – the number of columns. `LBound` is used in a similar manner to specify the lower limit.

ReDim

Sometimes we don't know in advance how big an array is going to be, for example when we are entering data into an array using a UserForm. The trick is to first `Dim` the array without a dimension,

```
Dim Company() As String
```

and then `ReDim` when we know the size, e.g.

```
ReDim Company(3)
```

If we wish to preserve the contents of the array however, we must include the `Preserve` keyword or else the contents will be lost, i.e.

```
ReDim Preserve Company(3)
```

This can be repeated, e.g. `ReDim Preserve Company(5)`.

When inputting data using an input box, an array size could be dynamically adjusted as more data is input. In the example below, an input box will appear each time with the prompt "Sales Figures?". As data is input, the array size is dynamically increased by one each time to accommodate the new element.

The Input box function shown here can only be used to input a String type. To be able to input other types and have more flexibility, we could use the InputBox method of the Application object. See the VBA Help for more details.

Multi dimensional arrays can be ReDimmed, but only the very last dimension can be changed when using ReDim with Preserve.

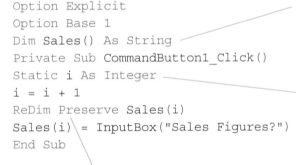

```
Option Explicit
Option Base 1
Dim Sales() As String
Private Sub CommandButton1_Click()
Static i As Integer
i = i + 1
ReDim Preserve Sales(i)
Sales(i) = InputBox("Sales Figures?")
End Sub
```

Sales is declared in the General Declarations

Since we are using a Static variable, its value is remembered from click to click

The ReDim statement ensures that the array size is increased by one each time

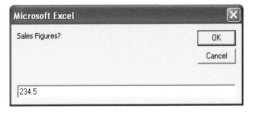

Variant arrays

An array, of course can hold `Variant` types, but also a single `Variant` variable can hold an array! A set of spreadsheet values can be assigned to a `Variant` in one line of code.

	A	B	
1	Business Systems	29 Highgrove rd	
2	Best Image	31 Curtin Ave	
3	Analytical Systems	28 Drayton Gdns	
4			

The following program segment will assign the values shown on the sheet above to the `Variant` variable `Company`, and arbitrarily display the first one.

When a Variant variable is assigned a range the resulting variant array is one-based.

```
Option Explicit
Private Sub CommandButton1_Click()
Dim Company As Variant
Company = Range("A1:B3").Value
MsgBox Company(1, 1)
End Sub
```

The array is assigned to a variant in one line

We can also do the reverse, i.e. fill a spreadsheet range with the values of a variant array – also in one line of code, e.g.

```
Range("C1:D3").Value = Company
```

Variant arrays always have two indices, even if they are assigned a single row or a single column.

We can put a `Variant` array variable (named `Titles` in this case) equal to a single *column* of values, e.g.

```
Dim Titles As Variant
Titles = Range("A1:A3").Value
```

In this case of course, the number of columns is one. So to access the 2nd element for example, we would use `Titles(2,1)`.

Similarly, if a `Variant` variable is assigned a row of values, the row number is always one. To access the 2nd element in the row, we would use `Titles(1,2)`.

The Array function

The `Array` function allows us to quickly and easily initialize a variant array. The code below initializes two variant arrays, `Company` and `Sales`.

```
Option Explicit
Private Sub CommandButton1_Click()
Dim Company As Variant, Sales As Variant
Company = Array("Business Systems", "Best Image", _
"Analytical Systems")
Sales = Array(2.34, 3.42, 5.62)
MsgBox Company(0)
MsgBox Sales(0)
End Sub
```

The Array function initializes a variant array which is zero-based by default.

The first elements have index 0. If Option Base were set to 1, the first element would have an index of 1

Arrays are faster

Generally speaking, another advantage of using arrays is that they can handle data more quickly than manipulating data on the spreadsheet. To that end, it is advantageous to read in the data from the spreadsheet to an array, perform the required operations on it, (e.g. sort it) and finally return it to the spreadsheet.

The UserForm

A UserForm is a customizable dialog box that can be used to input and display data. We will now make a very simple UserForm containing a list box which will display some company names.

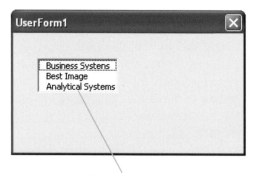

We will use a variant array in our code to hold the values used to populate this list box

To make a UserForm

From the VBE menu, click Insert, UserForm.

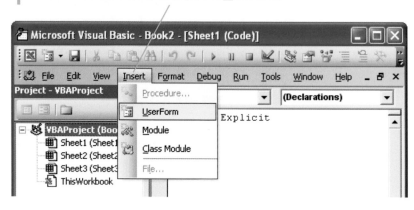

The UserForm designer appears (see over).

2   Click the ListBox control button on the UserForm ToolBox, and draw a list box on the form. View the Properties window and note the name of this list box (ListBox1).

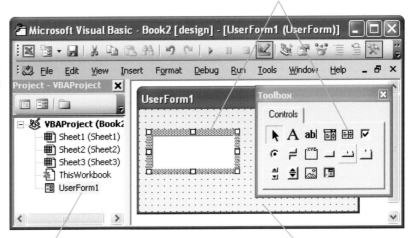

3   Note that the name of this UserForm is UserForm1. If, at any time we wish to return to the UserForm designer, double-click this name.

4   Double-click on the UserForm to access the UserForm's code module.

5   Ensure that UserForm is chosen in the Object box. Choose the Initialize event procedure in the drop-down and write the code shown.

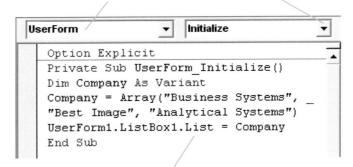

```
UserForm            Initialize

Option Explicit
Private Sub UserForm_Initialize()
Dim Company As Variant
Company = Array("Business Systems", _
"Best Image", "Analytical Systems")
UserForm1.ListBox1.List = Company
End Sub
```

The List property of the list box is used to populate the list box. It requires a variant array

6 Place a command button on the spreadsheet and place the code in it as shown, in order to simply display the UserForm.

```
Private Sub CommandButton1_Click()
UserForm1.Show
End Sub
```

7 To test the above code, return to the Excel sheet, exit design mode and click the command button. Our UserForm with its list box should appear as shown below. Click its Close button.

8 Return to the UserForm designer by double-clicking UserForm1 in Project Explorer from the VBE. Double-click the list box on the UserForm in order to access the ListBox1_Click event. Write the code shown below.

```
Private Sub ListBox1_Click()
MsgBox ListBox1.Value
MsgBox ListBox1.ListIndex
End Sub
```
ListIndex indicates the row number of the list box entry – starting with zero

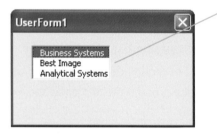

9 After making our UserForm appear once more (as per step 7, or by clicking the Run button in the VBE), click on one of the list box entries.

The ListIndex property could be used to access elements in arrays of values whose indices could correspond to the Company array index.

The list box's Value and ListIndex property values will be displayed

Run-time errors

Programming errors are of two main types, syntax and run-time. Syntax errors are those which occur at development time, e.g. omitting a Next in a For...Next loop. We have seen (only too often!) how these errors will be detected by the syntax checker – the program will not be allowed to run.

Run-time errors on the other hand, are errors which occur when the program is actually running. For example, consider this code segment which will divide 10 by the value in cell A1.

```
Private Sub CommandButton1_Click()
MsgBox 10 / Cells(1, 1).Value
End Sub
```

If there is a zero (or no value) in cell A1, a run-time error will occur and the following message will result:

Take note of the error number
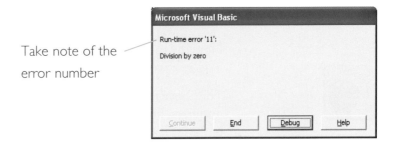

Whereas this is invaluable information to us as program developers, it is not what the user/customer wants to see. This run-time error reporting can be temporarily turned off by including On Error Resume Next before the offending line. This will cause program execution to continue undaunted after an offending error.

```
Private Sub CommandButton1_Click()
On Error Resume Next
MsgBox 10 / Cells(1, 1).Value
End Sub
```

In this case, with non-zero values, the result of the division will be displayed, whereas a division by zero will go unannounced, i.e. no message box! Such error "trapping" is automatically turned off when a procedure terminates. Alternatively, On Error GoTo 0 can be used to turn error trapping off.

The user could therefore be alerted, but not given the option of debugging or terminating the program by modifying the code as follows:

```
Private Sub CommandButton1_Click()
On Error Resume Next
MsgBox 10 / Cells(1, 1).Value
If Err.Number = 11 Then GoTo divZero
Exit Sub
divZero: MsgBox "A1 must contain a non-zero number"
End Sub
```

The line `If Err.Number = 11 Then GoTo divZero` causes control of the program to be transferred to the line with the label `divZero`. Label names are always followed by a colon. If an error ever occurs, the `Err` object is filled with information about the current error. `Number` is a property of this `Err` object which indicates the assigned number of the current error.

Note the use of `Exit Sub`, without which the line with label `divZero` would be executed, even if there were no error.

An error with Number 13 will result if text is inadvertently placed in cells(1,1) instead of a number and should also be accounted for in a practical version.

The above program code should work correctly for all non-zero numbers, but give an error message, as shown below if zero (or nothing) is entered into cell A1.

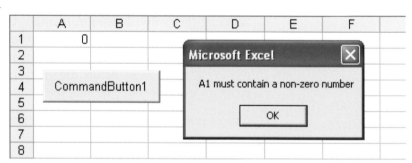

We could also use the `Description` property to describe the error, i.e. we could replace the corresponding line above with

```
divZero: MsgBox Err.Description
```

in which case we would get the message "Division by zero".

A run-time error will occur if we try to initialize an array element beyond the array's capacity. For example, if this code were run, an error message would result since element 3 does not exist.

```
Dim Sales(2) As Variant
Sales(3) = 32.34
```
"Subscript out of range" would result

If the user were for example, inputting array elements using an input box, we could write error trapping code to give an alert if too many entries were attempted.

```
Option Explicit
Option Base 1
Dim Sales(2) As Variant
Private Sub CommandButton1_Click()
On Error GoTo overRange
Static i As Integer
i = i + 1
Sales(i) = InputBox("Enter Sales")
Exit Sub
overRange: If Err.Number = 9 Then _
MsgBox "Only 2 entries allowed"
End Sub
```

An error number of 9 indicates "Subscript out of range"

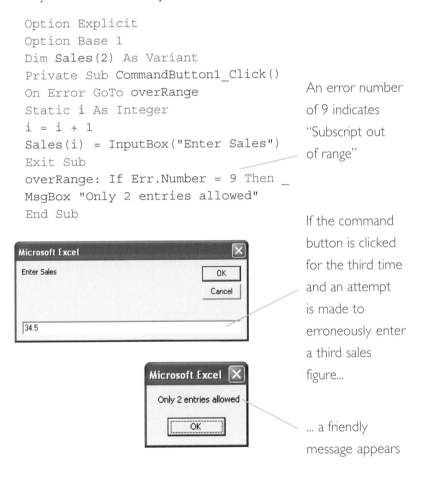

If the command button is clicked for the third time and an attempt is made to erroneously enter a third sales figure...

... a friendly message appears

Names

A Name defined in Excel (Insert, Name, Define...), e.g. "Sales" provides us with a way of communicating with Excel from VBA. We could refer to an Excel range from VBA using `Range("Sales")` for example.

This code will increase the values in a range named "Sales" by 10% and format the numbers correct to two decimal places.

```
Private Sub CommandButton1_Click()
Dim cl As Range
    For Each cl In Range("Sales")
    cl.Value = cl.Value * 1.1
    cl.NumberFormat = ".00"
    Next cl
End Sub
```

NumberFormat achieves the same effect as using the Format Cells dialog box from Excel (Format, Cells..., Number [tab], Custom)

Here is a novel way of storing your secret data in a Name which persists from session to session! First place some data in the range A1:A3. Clicking the first command button defines a Name (adds it to the workbook Names collection) called myName which stores a variant array, which itself contains the values in the range A1:A3. If the workbook is then closed and reopened (the values in the range A1:A3 having perhaps been deleted), the values are still available when the second command button is clicked!

```
Private Sub CommandButton1_Click()
Dim m As Variant
m = Range("A1:A3").Value        'variant array m
Names.Add Name:="myName", RefersTo:=m
End Sub
```

The Name containing the variant array is added to the Workbook Names collection

```
Private Sub CommandButton2_Click()
Dim n As Variant
n = [myName]
MsgBox n(2, 1)
End Sub
```

"Evaluate" ([ ]) is used to assign the values in the array to the variant n

The 2nd element in the array will be displayed

To add to the mystery, make the Name invisible by using Names.Add Name:="myName", RefersTo:=m, Visible:= False. To make it reappear in the Define Name dialog box, use Names("myName").Visible = True.

Date and Time

Excel already has an extensive range of functions which manipulate date and time. As well as being able to customize this functionality, VBA can extend it to provide extra capability.

Covers

Chapter Twelve

Now, Date and Time

Now

Even though Now() is a function, you may or may not include parentheses, i.e. MsgBox Now will suffice.

Now specifies the current date and time.

```
Private Sub CommandButton1_Click()
MsgBox Now()
End Sub
```

The format of the date actually displayed, US or otherwise, will depend upon the Windows Regional settings

To explicitly format a Date, use the Format function, e.g. MsgBox Format (Now, "mmmm") would display "September" in this case and MsgBox Format (Now, "mmm") would display "Sep". See VBA Help on the Format function.

The original intention was to make Jan 1 1900 day 1, i.e. Dec 31 1899 would be day 0, but unfortunately, somebody included Feb 29 in 1900 (not a leap year – see later), so Dec 30 1899 was subsequently made the start date.

Excel stores dates internally as a Date type (which is of the same 8-byte form as a Double type), the integral part of which is the number of days since Dec 30 1899, and the decimal part of which represents the fraction of the day after midnight.

Although dates are stored as decimal numbers, the way that we view them depends on how they are formatted. We can force a type conversion to a Double data type using:

```
Private Sub CommandButton1_Click()
MsgBox CDbl(Now)
End Sub
```

The VBA CDbl, ("convert to Double") function can be used to covert any data type (in this case the Date type) to a Double data type.

Number of days since Dec 30, 1899

Fraction of the day since midnight

Date and Time

The Date function returns only the current date without the time, e.g. MsgBox Date would display "09/09/2004" or similar (again the format displayed will depend on the Windows Regional setting), whereas MsgBox Time would return "15:53:20" or similar.

Separating date components

We use the correspondingly-named functions to extract the required parts as `Integer` values. Examples are given below.

Year, Month, Day

```
Private Sub CommandButton1_Click()
MsgBox Year(Date)
End Sub
```

Hour, Minute, Second

```
Private Sub CommandButton1_Click()
MsgBox Second(Time)
End Sub
```

Of course we could have used `Now` as an argument in both cases instead of `Date` and `Time` respectively.

DatePart

DatePart is also useful for working with year quarters, e.g. DatePart("q", Date) will return the present numeric quarter (1, 2, 3 or 4).

`DatePart` performs identically to the above functions, e.g. `DatePart("yyyy",Date)` would also extract the year as did `Year(Date)` above. It does have some special uses however, for example to find the day of the year:

```
Private Sub CommandButton1_Click()
MsgBox DatePart("y",Date)
End Sub
```

Today is the 253rd
day of this year

DateValue, TimeValue

These extract just the date and time components respectively, e.g.

```
Private Sub CommandButton1_Click()
MsgBox DateValue(Now)
End Sub
```

The date part only of the current date/time
is extracted (Identical to MsgBox Date)

Similarly, `TimeValue` would extract only the time part.

Assembling date components

DateSerial

Whereas `Year`, `Month`, etc. split a date into its components, `DateSerial` does the opposite. For example, `DateSerial(2004,12,1)` would form the date Dec 1, 2004. If a message box were used to output such a date, it would be presented according to your particular Windows Regional settings, i.e. either 12/1/2004 (US) or 1/12/2004 (UK).

Similarly, `MsgBox TimeSerial (1, 2, 3)` would display:

3 seconds after
2 minutes past 1

To find the date of first day of the current month use:

```
MsgBox DateSerial(Year(Date), Month(Date),1)
```

The date of the first day of the month of Sept 2004 (displayed here in US format). The present date in this case is 9/9/2004

Day 1

Date Delimiters

Without any delimiters, Excel VBA will perform a division, e.g. MsgBox 1/1/2000 will cause .0005 to be displayed.

CDate is even more versatile than DateValue. It will accept numerical arguments as well as Strings.

The number sign (#) can be used as a delimiter to enclose a `Date` type, e.g. `#10/30/98#`, but it must conform to the American format (mm/dd/yy). If it obviously doesn't, it will be changed before your eyes! For example, if `MsgBox Day(#30/10/98#)` is typed, it will immediately change. Due to this ambiguity, date literals are best avoided. Using double quotes as a delimiter, e.g. "10/30/98" also introduces ambiguity, as well as requiring an extra step to convert it to a date. To convert a `String` to a `Date`, use `DateValue`, e.g. `DateValue("December 1, 2004")`. As well as being preferable to using date literals, `DateValue` is forgiving of the format of the `String`, e.g. `MsgBox DateValue("Dec 1, 2004")` will display the date in a format determined by the Regional settings.

Adding and subtracting dates

Since the integer portion of a `Date` type represents the number of days, we can simply add or subtract an integral number of days to find another date, e.g. to find tomorrow's date we could use:

```
MsgBox DateValue(Now + 1)
```

DateAdd

To add intervals other than days, we must use `DateAdd`. For example, to work with weeks, use the "ww" interval code and to display the date one week hence use:

```
MsgBox DateAdd("ww", 1, Date)
```

The DateAdd interval code is "m" for months and "n" for minutes.

See the VBE Help for the other interval codes for `DateAdd`.

DateDiff

We can use `DateDiff` to find the number of days between two `Dates`. As well as taking into account the different lengths of the various months, `DateDiff` also takes into consideration the presence or absence of leap days between the two date intervals.

```
Private Sub CommandButton1_Click()
Dim strtDate As Date, fnshDate As Date
Dim n As Integer
strtDate = DateValue("Dec 1,2004")
fnshDate = DateValue("Mar 1,2005")
n = DateDiff("d", strtDate, fnshDate)
MsgBox n
End Sub
```

In the case of days, it would be possible to simply subtract the DateValues to find the difference.

The number of days between 00:00 hrs Dec 1, 2004 and 00:00 hrs "Mar 1, 2005" is 90

`DateDiff` can also be used to find the number of months between two dates for example, by changing the interval specifier to "m", e.g. `DateDiff("m", strtDate, fnshDate)`.

See Help on the `DateDiff` function for the other interval specifiers.

The number of weekdays

WeekDay

WeekDay will determine the day of the week as a number between 1 and 7 – where Sunday is 1 by default, e.g.

```
Private Sub CommandButton1_Click()
MsgBox Weekday(Date)
End Sub
```

In this case, today is Thursday – the 5th day of the week (with Sunday as day 1)

Microsoft Excel ☒
5
OK

We previously found the number of days between Dec 1 2004 and March 1 2005 to be 90. We now wish to find the number of *working* days (Monday to Friday) – perhaps for a project – between these two dates. March 1 2005 itself will this time be included.

```
Private Sub CommandButton1_Click()
Dim strtDate As Date, fnshDate As Date
Dim dt As Date, n As Long, i As Long
Dim numWorkDays As Long
strtDate = DateValue("Dec 1,2004")
fnshDate = DateValue("Mar 1,2005")
numWorkDays = 0
n = DateDiff("d", strtDate, fnshDate)
    For i = 0 To n          'n since March 1 is included
    dt = Weekday(strtDate + i)
    If (dt <> 7 And dt <> 1) Then
    numWorkDays = numWorkDays + 1
    End If
    Next i
MsgBox numWorkDays
End Sub
```

If not a Sat and not a Sun then...

...increment the number of workdays

We could omit DateDiff and modify the code, including the loop For i = strtDate to fnshDate, since these date values are integral.

Use VB built-in constants wherever possible to make your code more readable e.g. vbSunday and vbSaturday instead of 1 and 7.

The Internet is an invaluable source of VBA examples. Try typing "Excel VBA Date and Time" into your search engine.

The number of working days between project start and finish (inclusive) is 65

Microsoft Excel ☒
65
OK

As it stands, our program does not take account of any public holidays in the period, e.g. Christmas day. These would need to be explicitly, individually accounted for by the code.

The Mod operator

Mod gives the remainder after a division.

In this example 13 is divided by 3 (4 times) to give a remainder of 1 which would be displayed.

```
Private Sub CommandButton1_Click()
MsgBox 13 Mod 3
End Sub
```

Try MsgBox (1900 Mod 4 = 0) to confirm that it displays True.

Mod is an arithmetic operator, not a Date function but it could be used for example, to determine whether a year is leap or not. Mod can be used to determine whether a number is exactly divisible, e.g. 1900 Mod 4 would return 0, indicating that 1900 was exactly divisible by 4.

We could also determine if a year is leap by testing if Month(DateSerial (yr, 2, 29)) = 2, which seems to be forgiving of the bogus 1900 leap year!

This would suggest that the year 1900 was a leap year, since it is divisible by 4, but in addition, in 1582, Pope Gregory decreed, that years divisible by 100 were *not* to be leap years. If a variable yr were 1900 or 2000 for example, also stipulating that (yr Mod 100) <> 0, i.e. yr is not divisible by 100, would rule out 1900 and 2000 since they are.

However, to further compensate for the earth's non-exact rotation, the good Pope decreed that every 400 years *was* to be a leap year, i.e. if we also allow the condition yr Mod 400 = 0, i.e. yr could be divisible by 400, 2000 would now qualify, but 1900 would not. Combining these conditions into one logical expression, we could test for a leap year (e.g. 1900) using:

And will evaluate to False if either expression evaluates to False. Or will evaluate to True if either expression evaluates to True. Try MsgBox (True And False Or False) to confirm that it displays False.

```
Private Sub CommandButton1_Click()
Dim yr As Integer
yr = 1900
MsgBox (yr Mod 4 = 0) And (yr Mod 100 <> 0) _
Or (yr Mod 400 = 0)
End Sub
```

True for 1900

To test the code further, try changing yr to 1901, 1904, 2000, etc.

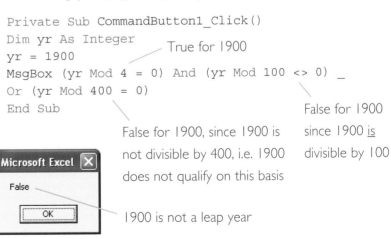

False for 1900, since 1900 is not divisible by 400, i.e. 1900 does not qualify on this basis

False for 1900 since 1900 <u>is</u> divisible by 100

1900 is not a leap year

Anniversaries

To find your age, you could subtract the year of your birth from the present year.

The only problem is that you may or may not have had your birthday yet this year. If you haven't had your birthday, you will need to subtract a year. How do we determine if you have had your birthday this year or not? We need to test whether today's date (Date) is less than the date of your birthday this year.

The date of your birthday this year will be given by `DateSerial(Year(Date), Month(dob), Day(dob))`, where dob is your date of birth, i.e. your date of birth with the current year substituted for your year of birth, so `Date < DateSerial(Year(Date), Month(dob), Day(dob))` will be `True` if your birthday has yet to come this year.

This program should display your age if you use your date of birth.

```
Private Sub CommandButton1_Click()
Dim age As Integer
Dim dob As Date, bday As Date
dob = DateValue("Oct 30, 1966")
bday = DateSerial(Year(Date), Month(dob), Day(dob))
age = Year(Date) - Year(dob) + (Date < bday)
MsgBox age & " years old"
End Sub
```

Microsoft Excel

37 years old

OK

(Date < bday) will have the numeric value of -1 (True) if your birthday has not yet passed, and 0 (False) if it has

True has the Integer value of -1, whereas False has the Integer value of 0. Try using the VBA conversion function CInt (which converts any given data type – in this case a Boolean – into an Integer data type) by using MsgBox CInt(False) and MsgBox CInt(True) to confirm this.

Speaking of birthdays, you could determine the day of the week that you were born using this code with your date of birth.

```
Private Sub CommandButton1_Click()
Dim dob As Date
dob = DateValue("Oct 30, 1966")
MsgBox Format(dob, "dddd")
End Sub
```

Microsoft Excel

Sunday

OK

The Application object

The Application object represents Excel itself. As well as
having many useful general purpose properties and methods,
the Application object gives access to the many well-known
Excel worksheet functions.

Covers

Chapter Thirteen

Application properties

The `Application` object is the parent of all objects in the Excel Object Model.

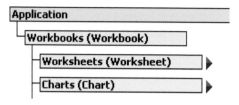

Option settings

Since it represents the entire Excel application, the `Application` object can give access to many of the application-wide settings of the Excel Tools, Options... dialog box. For example, we can set the number of worksheets in a (new) workbook using the `SheetsInNewWorkbook` property as follows:

```
Private Sub CommandButton1_Click()
Application.SheetsInNewWorkbook = 5
End Sub
```

If this code is run and a new workbook opened, it will contain five worksheets as shown below.

StatusBar

This property is used to set the text which appears on the status bar at the bottom left of the screen.

```
Private Sub CommandButton1_Click()
Application.StatusBar = "Calculating..."
End Sub
```

When the code is run, the text will appear in the status bar of the Excel window

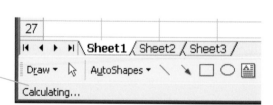

ScreenUpdating

To avoid screen flicker and make your code run faster, the screen can be frozen when your code is running using:

```
Application.ScreenUpdating = False
```

Whereas ScreenUpdating will revert to True automatically when the code terminates, it is good practise to do this explicitly with:

```
Application.ScreenUpdating = True
```

DisplayAlerts

Under normal circumstances, when we close a workbook, we will be asked for confirmation if changes have been made.

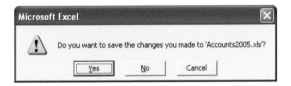

If DisplayAlerts is set to False, this dialog box is suppressed, and any changes are lost, as running this code will demonstrate.

```
Private Sub CommandButton1_Click()
Application.DisplayAlerts = False
ActiveWorkbook.Close
Application.DisplayAlerts = True
End Sub
```

Returning DisplayAlerts to True is not essential since it will be done automatically on exit from the procedure

Some Application properties are "globals", and don't require to be preceded with Application, e.g. rather than Application.Selection, we can just use Selection on its own.

Try running the above code after making a change to a sheet. Reopen the workbook and note that the changes have not been saved.

Setting DisplayAlerts to False is particularly useful if we wish to avoid the possibility of a user canceling an operation whilst code is running, thereby possibly avoiding subsequent code conflict.

WorkSheetFunction

We can access most of Excel's worksheet functions using VBA's `WorkSheetFunction`.

Sum

For example, we can obtain the *result* of Excel's SUM function shown here, by using the code shown beneath. Note that the formula itself is not inserted.

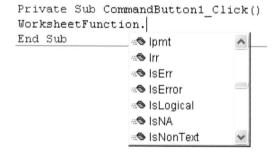

```
Private Sub CommandButton1_Click()
Cells(4, 1).Value = _
WorksheetFunction.Sum(Range("A1:A3"))
End Sub
```

Take note that the argument of Sum is a Range object – not a String

To determine which of the Excel worksheet functions are available, type "`WorksheetFunction.`" into your VBE editor and scroll through the IntelliSense suggestions which appear.

```
Private Sub CommandButton1_Click()
WorksheetFunction.
End Sub
```

- Ipmt
- Irr
- IsErr
- IsError
- IsLogical
- IsNA
- IsNonText

Many Excel functions are duplicated in VBA and serve the same purpose, e.g. Excel's ABS and VBA's `Abs`. Some are not represented at all, e.g. the Excel CONCATENATE is not available from VBA using the `WorkSheetFunction` object since VBA has a perfectly good & operator to concatenate strings.

PMT

To get Help on worksheet functions such as PMT, consult Excel Help, not VBA Help.

From VBA we can access the PMT Excel worksheet function which will allow us to calculate mortgage payments. For example, we could calculate the monthly payments on $100,000 over 20 years at 5% interest using:

```
Private Sub CommandButton1_Click()
Dim rate As Double, nper As Integer
Dim paymnt As Double
rate = 0.05 / 12: nper = 20 * 12
paymnt = WorksheetFunction.Pmt(rate, nper, 100000)
MsgBox paymnt
End Sub
```

Note that `rate` is the rate per period, i.e. the *monthly* interest rate which is the annual interest rate divided by 12, and `nper` is the total number of monthly payments over 20 years, i.e. 20 x 12.

A negative value indicates that payment must be made

If it is desirable to present this result as a positive value correct to two decimal places, for `MsgBox paymnt` we could substitute:

```
MsgBox Format(Abs(paymnt), ".##")
```

Abs will return positive values only

".##" will format correct to 2 decimal places, but compared with ".00" will not insert 0 placeholders

The payment would then be displayed as shown:

Methods

OnTime

OnTime allows us to run some code at a time of our choosing.

Chose Insert, Module from the VBE menu to insert a standard code module.

1. Create a procedure in a standard code module that we wish to run some time in the future.

```
Sub mBox()
MsgBox "Sub called"
End Sub
```

2. Write the code shown below which will automatically call the mBox sub three seconds after the command button is clicked.

```
Private Sub CommandButton1_Click()
Application.OnTime Now() + _
  TimeSerial(0, 0, 3), "mBox"
End Sub
```

TimeSerial returns a time of 0 hours, 0 minutes and 3 seconds

The name of the procedure to be run

Procedures that are called by OnTime and OnKey must be written in a standard code module.

Three seconds after the command button is clicked, this message box appears

OnKey

OnKey allows us to run a procedure by simply pressing a key. For example, after this code is run, we could subsequently run the mBox procedure (assuming that it is in the standard code module) by simply pressing the Tab key.

Since the command button will have the focus after running this code, it is necessary to click back on the worksheet before pressing the Tab key (or alternatively, set the CommandButton's TakeFocusOnClick property to False).

```
Private Sub CommandButton1_Click()
Application.OnKey "{TAB}", "mBox"
End Sub
```

To return the Tab key to its default functionality, use:

```
Application.OnKey "{TAB}"
```

Undo

Undo will undo the last action taken by the user. Here's a novel program which saves values that you overtype. It places the overtyped value in a cell to the right. In this case, Undo causes the typed-over value to temporarily reappear in the same cell.

Take care that there is no important data in the cell to the right!

When using a Worksheet_Change event which itself changes the contents of a cell, Application.EnableEvents should be set to False in the procedure, lest a chain reaction occurs.

```
Private Sub Worksheet_Change(ByVal Target As Range)
Dim x As Variant
Application.EnableEvents = False
x = Target.Value                The new value entered is saved in x
Application.Undo
Target.Offset(, 1).Value = Target.Value
Target.Value = x
Application.EnableEvents = True          After the Undo,
End Sub                                  Target.Value will
                                         hold the old value
         Target.Value = x causes         which is then placed
         the saved (typed-in) value      in the cell one
         to be returned to the cell      column to the right
```

After a new number is entered into a cell, the overtyped value will appear in the cell to the right

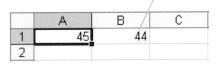

The selection will not be seen to move down (or whatever was the default action) on pressing Enter, since that operation was also undone. Target.Offset(1).Select could be used to move it down.

SendKeys

The SendKeys statement can be used in code to send keystrokes to Excel. The effect is exactly the same as physically pressing the corresponding key/s on the keyboard.

For example, the Alt+h key combination from the Excel window causes the Help menu to drop down. The VBA code

```
SendKeys "%h"
```

Whereas it is possible to call Excel functions from the Excel menu using SendKeys, it is considered something of a last resort.

would have exactly the same effect.

The % character represents the Alt key. See Help for others.

Volatile

A volatile function is one which is automatically called when a sheet is *recalculated*. UDFs (user defined functions) are not volatile by default. Consider this UDF which simply displays the name of the active sheet in a cell. Type the UDF shown below into a standard code module (as described on page 156):

```
Function GetWorksheetName() As Variant
GetWorksheetName = ActiveSheet.Name
End Function
```

The sheet name will appear in cell A1 when the function is entered

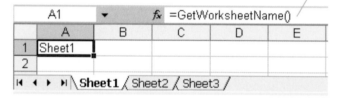

Unfortunately, if the worksheet name is now *changed*, whereby a recalculation is deemed to have occurred, the UDF will not automatically trigger, and the new name will not be displayed in cell A1. Try it.

To remedy this, include `Application.Volatile` as the first line in the UDF as shown below:

```
Function GetWorksheetName() As Variant
Application.Volatile
GetWorksheetName = ActiveSheet.Name
End Function
```

Now the new name is displayed at once in cell A1 when the sheet name is changed, thereby demonstrating that our UDF is volatile

Index

G

H

I

K

L

M

N

P

O

R

R1C1 style   59
Rand   186
Range   11, 56, 87, 108, 111
Read, Property   58, 85
ReDim   161
RefersTo   170
Regional settings   172
Registry   72
Require Variable Declaration   21
Resize   119, 121
RGB function   62
Right   50
RightFooter   102
Row, Property   81, 126
Rows   81, 84–85, 109
Run-time   129
Run-time errors   167–169

S

Scope   150
ScreenUpdating   181
Second   173
Security setting   12
Select   54, 63, 71, 84, 108
Select Case   38, 66
Selection   60, 111, 115, 120, 126, 131, 152, 181
SelectionChange   86–87, 124
SendKeys   185
Set   63
SheetDeactivate   101
SheetSelectionChange   99–100
SheetsInNewWorkbook   180
Single   22, 26
Single step   31
SmallChange   136

Spin button   135
SpinDown   135
SpinUp   135
Static   153, 161, 169
StatusBar   180
Step Into   31
Stop button   14
Stop Recording button   69
Str   18, 28, 66, 149
String   13, 16
String handling   50–52
Sub   11, 16, 144–152, 154
Sum   109, 182
Swap variables   17
Syntax error   13, 167

T

Tab   41, 184
TakeFocusOnClick   61, 65, 184
Target   87–89
Task bar   11
Text box control   133–134
TextBox object   134
ThisWorkbook   99–100, 102
Time   172
TimeSerial   174, 184
TimeValue   173
Toolbar, to run a macro from   77
Trim   49
True   22, 37, 42, 177
Type, Variable   16
Type-declaration characters   23
TypeName   105

U

V

W

X

Y